Editor-in-Chief and Founder:
  Lyndon H. LaRouche, Jr.
Editorial Board: *Lyndon H. LaRouche, Jr. , Helga Zepp-LaRouche, Paul Gallagher, Tony Papert, Gerald Rose, Dennis Small, Jeffrey Steinberg, William Wertz*
Co-Editors: *Paul Gallagher, Tony Papert*
Managing Editor: *Nancy Spannaus*
Technology: *Marsha Freeman*
Books: *Katherine Notley*
Ebooks: *Richard Burden*
Graphics: *Alan Yue*
Photos: *Stuart Lewis*
Circulation Manager: *Stanley Ezrol*

INTELLIGENCE DIRECTORS
Counterintelligence: *Jeffrey Steinberg, Michele Steinberg*
Economics: *John Hoefle, Marcia Merry Baker, Paul Gallagher*
History: *Anton Chaitkin*
Ibero-America: *Dennis Small*
Russia and Eastern Europe: *Rachel Douglas*
United States: *Debra Freeman*

INTERNATIONAL BUREAUS
Bogotá: *Miriam Redondo*
Berlin: *Rainer Apel*
Copenhagen: *Tom Gillesberg*
Houston: *Harley Schlanger*
Lima: *Sara Madueño*
Melbourne: *Robert Barwick*
Mexico City: *Gerardo Castilleja Chávez*
New Delhi: *Ramtanu Maitra*
Paris: *Christine Bierre*
Stockholm: *Ulf Sandmark*
United Nations, N.Y.C.: *Leni Rubinstein*
Washington, D.C.: *William Jones*
Wiesbaden: *Göran Haglund*

ON THE WEB
e-mail: eirns@larouchepub.com
www.larouchepub.com
www.executiveintelligencereview.com
www.larouchepub.com/eiw
Webmaster: *John Sigerson*
Assistant Webmaster: *George Hollis*
Editor, Arabic-language edition: *Hussein Askary*

EIR (ISSN 0273-6314) *is published weekly (50 issues), by EIR News Service, Inc., P.O. Box 17390, Washington, D.C. 20041-0390. (703) 777-9451*

European Headquarters: E.I.R. GmbH, Postfach Bahnstrasse 9a, D-65205, Wiesbaden, Germany
Tel: 49-611-73650
Homepage: http://www.eirna.com
e-mail: eirna@eirna.com
Director: Georg Neudecker

Montreal, Canada: 514-461-1557

Denmark: EIR - Danmark, Sankt Knuds Vej 11, basement left, DK-1903 Frederiksberg, Denmark. Tel.: +45 35 43 60 40, Fax: +45 35 43 87 57. e-mail: eirdk@hotmail.com.

Mexico City: EIR, Sor Juana Inés de la Cruz 242-2 Col. Agricultura C.P. 11360 Delegación M. Hidalgo, México D.F. Tel. (5525) 5318-2301 eirmexico@gmail.com

Postmaster: Send all address changes to *EIR*, P.O. Box 17390, Washington, D.C. 20041-0390.

Signed articles in *EIR* represent the views of the authors, and not necessarily those of the Editorial Board.

We Need
A New FDR Recovery

EIR Contents

www.larouchepub.com Volume 42, Number 35, September 4, 2015

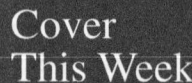

©TVA

Cover This Week

The Sequoyah Nuclear Plant, one of the three nuclear complexes which are part of FDR's Tennessee Valley Authority

Platonic Dialogue in Manhattan On Saturday, August 29, 2015

Dennis Speed: My name is Dennis Speed and on behalf of the LaRouche Political Action Committee I want to welcome everybody to today's continued dialogue with Lyndon LaRouche. I want to begin today by quoting Jonathan Swift, who said, "When a true genius appears in the world, you may know him by this sign, that the dunces are all in confederacy against him." That principle of the confederacy is the one that Alexander Hamilton successfully eliminated, in the Presidency that he created together with George Washington, here in this city.

Lyndon LaRouche in video-discussion with the Manhattan Project on August 29, 2015.

larouchepac.com

And so, as everybody knows who's been coming to these meetings, and everybody will find out who has not, the issue of the Presidency and the removal of Barack Obama is a function of what we here do, and we here do in Manhattan. So without further comments, I'm going to ask Lyn if you have anything you want to say before we start right in with the questions?

LaRouche's Opening Statement

I think that what's important here, is the fact that during the recent weeks that we've been assembled here, we have reached into an area which is absolutely awesome. It's not just what we're doing, it's what the situation is: We're now coming to the countdown which is going to determine whether or not we are able to save humanity from a serious threat of conflict; or whether we're going to go down

with it. And I think we should devote ourselves to the relevance of things that may bear on getting out of this mess, rather than waiting for it to envelop us. And I think that's where we are right now.

Q: Before I speak, I want to draw everyone's attention to the information that we got today. Mr. LaRouche has a statement within that information that everybody should take a look at, and memorize—no, you don't have to memorize it. [laughter] OK, but it's here, it's in our packet: It says, "Wall Street Is Hopelessly Bankrupt, Institute Glass-Steagall Worldwide Immediately." This is Mr. LaRouche's statement.

And what I wanted to say—good afternoon, Mr. LaRouche, how are you?

LaRouche: Not too bad.

Q: [follow-up] You look great! OK! Mr. LaRouche, you have issued a statement calling for worldwide Glass-Steagall. Now, next week, there will be a major meeting of the United Nations General Assembly in New York City. It is said that President Putin of Russia and Xi Jinping of China will be in attendance at these proceedings; and these nations, China and Russia, among others, are acutely aware of the war danger. But you have emphasized that the war danger is being driven by the financial crisis, and the only solution, in addition to the immediate impeachment of Obama, is Glass-Steagall, in the United States and worldwide.

Now, as a Manhattan Project person, and many

people here are part of that Manhattan Project, I would like your suggestions on how we are to make it known that this important meeting is taking place; in the past, we have been to the missions that are associated with the countries that are in the General Assembly. We have given information to them and spoken to people in high rank at the missions of these countries, that are located in Manhattan.

I would say, first of all, this is an auspicious coincidence, shall we say, that what the issue is now, is the manner of how we are going to throw a President out of office. Because this President, if he were to remain in office, and he's demonstrated his direction in that connection, would be a threat to the continued existence of not only the people of the United States, but also the people of the planet.

But in addition to that, or maybe you wanted to talk a little more about that, but what would be your suggestions for us, to make this meeting known?

What Kind of Evil Would Do This?

LaRouche: I would say, first of all, this is an auspicious coincidence, shall we say, that what the issue is now, is the manner of how we are going to throw a President out of office. Because this President, if he were to remain in office, and he's demonstrated his directions in that connection, would be a threat to the continued existence of not only the people of the United States, but also the people of the planet.

This is something particularly evil. We see reflections of that in terms of what we see in the mass deaths in Europe. We have these whole areas where people come out of the swamps or the deserts of the area; and they struggle to escape from northern Africa, these areas of northern Africa and so forth. And they are murdered in large numbers, by drowning or other measures now.

So the point now, is that we have to think about, what is the kind of *evil* which would do these things? And one of them is Obama. And Obama is not just something unto himself. He's a figure,—his father, or his nominal father was a very evil person, and this guy is also a very evil person. But you don't just go around killing evil persons. What you have to do, is you have to unleash, from mankind itself, the ability to recognize what they have to do, to *free themselves* from this; what

actions they should take, what dedication they should have, what positive intentions they have, to bring this about.

And I would say, right now, and it's not an exaggeration in any sense; I'm being a somewhat old man, as they say, in the trades these days, I've lived a long life; I probably will a little more, if I shut my mouth, I guess, and avoid these dangers. [laughter] But the point is, that we in this area represent a part of the United States of Alexander Hamilton. And the Hamilton tradition, based in Manhattan, essentially; he was also in other parts of the place, but that was he. Because he is the one who has inspired,—despite all the evil that has gone on inside the United States in its history,—he is the one person whose mind reminds us of what our mission is: A dedication to bring about the good, in order to get rid of the devil. And that's what I think we are.

And I think that this location, this, in Manhattan, is important because there's something left of Alexander Hamilton, which is still alive inside this area, not just down in the place in the bottom of the area. But this is great. And we think, what the teaching profession has been in Manhattan, and what the best teachers have been; they weren't always given the best shot at doing the job, but they represent a body of people who represent one of the highest standards of education of young people, *despite* the rundown of the education system so far. We used to have a better education system, *But!* we have teachers who are dedicated to that intention, and that makes this place special!

Q: I'm K__ from the Bronx. George Washington had said, trade with other nations, but do not get involved in their politics. And at the time they were forming the UN, someone said it will give people an opportunity to come together to fight, or maybe he said "quarrel," but to show their displeasures with each other.

Our elite, parasitical class has been bringing us together in a one-world situation, so that we can all think the same thing; and I don't know if they ever intended for us to get along, but that was supposedly the idea.

Shortly before I left the house this morning, I found something on there that was of great interest to me: There is a nationalist sentiment spreading around the world, and I wonder if you could comment on it.

When Hillary Clinton Caved

But before you do, I understand that Hungary is building a 110-mile, 13-foot high wall around there, a fence or a wall; and I understand Bulgaria is building a 50-foot steel fence around them, and that this is something that's going to take place in many more places, that it's going to spread around. This country has shown an interest in also eliminating the people coming in from the border; it isn't that we don't welcome people in this country, it's that we feel that it's overwhelming us. Can you comment on the nationalist sentiment that is starting to build?

LaRouche: I certainly can. And with fulsome feelings and knowledge of the matter. This is a product largely of the administration of Obama, President Obama. What happened, is when Obama caused the murder of four representatives of the United States in that territory [Libya], Obama lied, and said the thing had to do with some crazy mystic from that part of the world. He lied!

But a certain woman who was involved with this process flinched! She knew he was lying. She knew that he was guilty of the assassination of these representatives of the Presidency of the United States. That was Hillary Clinton. She knew that. She was working under Obama at that time. And four of these people, officials of the United States, were killed, under the order of Obama. And Hillary Clinton balked; she was still a member of the staff of Obama and she flinched and balked, and caved in to Obama.

And she's living through a very terrible life right now, psychologically, because she knows all this. Her husband, Bill Clinton, is stymied by the horror of what her position represents now, because this is becoming more and more acute; because Obama's Satanic qualities are becoming increasingly manifest. We have a Congress which in general will not move on this issue. We have more and more people prepared to support Obama in launching a *war* which could cause, as a result, could cause the extermination of the human species.

Obama's Murders: The burning of the U.S. consulate in Benghazi, Libya on September 11, 2012.

rt/youtube

And so we're in a time like that, where we have to do something about it. How do we do that? Well, the first thing is not that we have muscles or power of that sort. The point is our willpower, or creative impulses, truly creative impulses. That we have to understand the situation, recognize it, and create a movement inside our own society to make sure that Obama is told, under the 25th Amendment, to get the hell out of here. That's our best shot.

Q: I went through that period, I'm sure you did, because our ages are close to the same, where we had that crash in 1933. My family and I had come through the transition of gas lights and kerosene lanterns for illumination; thanks be to God, to Thomas Edison who brought us out of that darkness.

I want to state that I've been troubled by many things that have gone on in the world today, particularly the antics of Wall Street. We definitely need to combat that group of individuals who are seeking nothing but money for themselves at the expense of the United States of America. Surely, you're aware of that.

LaRouche: Yeah! Well, I don't know how my age compares with you, but I think we had some similar experiences in some past years ago.

It's understandable. What you're saying is understandable to me, totally. We went through the effects of the 1920s. We went through the effects of the 1930s, which were much better under Franklin Roosevelt. And things got pretty bad after Franklin Roosevelt died, because the wrong people got into power. And that stuff.... We had a couple of Kennedys, and they were

But the point is, that we in this area represent a part of the United States of Alexander Hamilton. And the Hamilton tradition, based in Manhattan, essentially; he was also in other parts of the place, but that was he. Because he is the one who has inspired,—despite all the evil that has gone on inside the United States in its history,—he is the one person whose mind reminds us of what our mission is: A dedication to bring about the good, in order to get rid of the devil. And that's what I think we are.

pretty good people. We had also two leading commanders in military affairs, like MacArthur and others during the war period and afterward.

But we also had some very bad people brought into the power over the United States' policy during those years. We had Presidents who were very good, and we had Presidents who were *very* bad. And now we're at a point where I will say, after, shall we say, the 1980s and the beginning of the 1990s, apart from Bill Clinton—apart from Bill Clinton!—everything was going to Hell since that time.

We Kept Going Down and Down

And we have to stop that now. We have to realize that some of us, especially older people, who still remember a little bit about the history of the United States in the Twentieth Century, have the means of the *insight* to realize what the nature of the thing is we have to deal with. We, as old people, like me, we have to do our part in ensuring that the coming generations make it, and we don't go into a thermonuclear war which threatens the existence of the human species, which is what Obama threatens. Obama's operation is a threat to the existence of the human species. And let's hope that enough people in this world understand that we have to stop that. Pull him out, 25th Amendment. Throw him out. That's it.

Q: [follow-up] Unfortunately, we lost a tremendous asset that was Franklin Delano Roosevelt, who saved our bacon and put us back on the road to recovery. I can recall that vividly, where he instituted several organizations like CCC camps, where some of my relatives were able to get suitable employment, so they could survive, and my family could survive. And I classify him as one of our greatest Presidents. I'll never forget him.

I could talk on more. You're aware of what I am saying and God bless you, sir. Continue in your endeavor. I've been following you for a *good number* of years. I have found no fault in you whatsoever. Continue in your courageous work. God bless you, sir.

LaRouche: Thank you.

Q: Hi, Lyn, it's A__ from New York. I wanted to ask you or bring to your attention and get some feedback from you on what appears to be now in the population, but in amongst the leadership as well, the desire to sidestep, try and dance away, divert the subject from both Glass-Steagall and the threat of nuclear war. When you talk to people, they'll say "Well, yeah, we know about Iran." That kind of thing, as if that is the type of silly issue that is threatening them.

You know that they're not important, but this is typified by organizations like Moveon.org and so on. I understand that demonstrations are being organized against Schumer; so this type of silliness is happening on various levels. I think those of us here don't have a problem dealing with people face to face and head on, and presenting what is real and what they need to pay attention to. But with these types of dangerous silliness going on, I was wondering what you could speak more about that, and perhaps there's an even more direct way that we should handle this.

LaRouche: I think there's a deeper one that has to be considered. Some things are things that were buried under the ground, so to speak, over more than a century, in the Twentieth Century, for example. And what happened then, you had President Roosevelt, Franklin Roosevelt as President; this was actually a bonanza, in particular, for the United States. But then he died, and the day—and there's this picture which I know of, sort of, directly, that the President, Franklin Roosevelt, was in the last moments of his life, and two friends of mine, one a prominent official, military, and another official, who I later came to work with closely in the later part of my own career; that we lost what Franklin Roosevelt represented,—it was taken away from us.

Yes, we had war heroes, we had important people, important figures, who after Roosevelt's death, and also for Presidents of that period, they benefitted. But gradually it got worse and worse; we kept going down and down and down; we got worse and worse. We became more stupid, more blocked, more intimidated. We quit.

We have to realize that some of us, especially older people, who still remember a little bit about the history of the United States in the Twentieth Century, have the means of the insight to realize what the nature of the thing is we have to deal with. We, as old people, like me, we have to do our part in ensuring that the coming generations make it, and we don't go into a thermonuclear war which threatens the existence of the human species, which is what Obama threatens. Obama's operation is a threat to the existence of the human species. And let's hope that enough people in this world understand that we have to stop that. Pull him out, 25th Amendment. Throw him out. That's it.

We stopped fighting, as we should fight. We should fight for principle—it's fight for war, it's fight for principle—to ensure that the nation and its people will have access to a program of action for the development of the human species, for our nation; and that has been down.

And as a matter of fact, this is not something new. This is old. With the beginning of the Twentieth Century, the United States came under subjugation of Bertrand Russell, a purely evil man, one of the most evil men in all history, since that time. And at the same time, we used to actually practice science. The greatest scientists we had in the United States and in Europe, for example, were great scientists. And their work was tremendous. But what happened is, because of the influence of Russell, Bertrand Russell, the most evil man of the century, at that time, Russell's influence corrupted and almost destroyed science. We are now teaching mathematics, not physical science.

Obama the Greatest Threat to Humanity

And what happened is, in the course of this process, up to the Twentieth Century, we got to a problem where most of the scientists of the Twentieth Century have rejected science. They use mathematics, not science. Einstein, Albert Einstein, was one of the exceptional people, who in his own lifetime, maintained the principle of science.

We have in various parts of the world people who are truly scientists, but we have fewer and fewer of them. Our education system is being corrupted. We no longer have any connection of any significance. Our children, our generations of children, are becoming more and more ignorant, more and more like savages, lacking morality, lacking a meaning of life.

And therefore, the thing we have to do, we have to understand, like old men like me, we have to understand that we have a responsibility to turn the tide and to bring *science*, true science, rather than cheapo tricks,

in order to bring mankind *back* to the course of action which the United States had followed, in the best years of our life, as in the United States. And that's where we are.

So, now on this occasion, here we are. Obama is the greatest threat to humanity on the planet. Not because he's acting against foreigners, but because he is the evil person, he is the evil force. He is the thing that has to be kicked out by the 25th Amendment, and kicked out of office right now. Because Obama is determined, now, to launch a thermonuclear war across the trans-Atlantic region. And if that war occurs, you'll have the kind of warfare which Obama intends to bring about, now, and that would cause a general extermination of the human species. In other words, the general assumption is, that if Obama and the British, who created him, if they were able to do this, and they *are* able to do it, then there would be very few people left on this planet. And this could happen in one day!

And that's where we are, and therefore we do have a real mission; we have a mission to get people to arouse themselves and to realize that this *is* the circumstance. And if the human will, the will of our citizens, could muster a significant part of itself to face the truth of this matter, I guarantee you, that many people, as in New York City, would say, "No! No! it's not going to happen." And we need Obama thrown out of office, thrown back where he belongs, with the 25th Amendment. [applause]

Q: Good afternoon, Mr. LaRouche, are you hearing me? My question is, gun violence in the United States is out of control. How can we stop the gun violence here? How can we solve this problem?

Obama's Mass Murders

LaRouche: Fine. Well, the problem here is, this is being promoted. You have to look at the other side of this thing, take a foreign case; in order to look at what's

youtube

Obama's Murders: The recovery of bodies of refugees drowned in the Mediterranean Sea off the coast of Libya.

going on in the United States, sometimes you have to look to foreign nations, because you have look there to see if there's something going on in foreign nations, which gives you a key to what the problem is inside the United States. In other words, you want to have an objective view, not just an impression.

Now, the fact of the matter is, the greatest horror that's going on right now, is that Obama set into motion, under his operations in various parts of the foreign areas, mass killing. And therefore what he's done, and he's brought this into the United States, he's really been an assassin. He's also destroyed our economy. He played a very specific role in all that.

Now the solution for us, the peaceful solution for dealing with Obama, who is the chief threat to the existence of the people of the United States, along with other peoples: Take the 25th Amendment of the United States. As a law, that law provides for Obama being removed from the Presidency on a short notice, and taking him out *permanently from any authority in the United States, and elsewhere.*

What Obama is doing: in Africa, he has orchestrated a system of assassination in various African nations, North Africa, other adjacent areas, and this is resulting in

> What happens in the United States in terms of poor employment, and all these things? That's all there. But you want to see the heart of it, look at what's going on there in Europe, the people who are being mass killed in Europe; driven from Africa, and they drown in the sea. If they landed in Europe, somebody was waiting to mass kill them, 70, 80 people at a time; suddenly they're found dead, among these people who are trying to emigrate to safety in Europe. This is the situation.

mass deaths in these areas. Obama's operation terrifies people in Northern Africa and other locations, in the Middle East. Now what happened, the people become terrified because of what's going on from Obama. Obama's pressure then pushes people from North Africa and adjacent areas, and pushes them into a mass drive to get across the sea there, in order to escape Northern Africa.

When they go onto the sea, somebody's out there ready to kill them, by sinking boats which are overloaded. They land inside Europe. What happens there? They become murdered! They are looking for a place to live, safe from those forces which Obama has set forth into Northern Africa. They get there, and they find they're being received by people in Europe, who want to kill them. Not that everybody does it, but there is a very significant amount of killing of people who are dumped onto the sea waters; they're drowned because of accidents, forced accidents; they were starved; but they kept coming and coming, because they were trying to escape the *terror* which Obama's operation in Northern Africa has created!

So this is not a practical problem in the ordinary sense. This is a criminal action beyond belief. And it is Barack Obama, the President of the United States, who is responsible for the biggest part of this problem. And that's what the real problem is.

Well, what happens in the United States in terms of poor employment, and all these things? That's all there. But you want to see the heart of it, look at what's going on there in Europe, the people who are being mass killed in Europe; driven from Africa, and they drown in the sea. If they landed in Europe, somebody was waiting to mass kill them, 70, 80 people at a time; suddenly they're found dead, among these people who are trying to emigrate to safety in Europe. This is the situation.

So what you're talking about, yes, is a valid concern. But it doesn't come close to what Obama is causing to occur in Europe, and around Europe, and inside the United States itself. We have a good cause, and we have to muster ourselves to make sure that cause is successful. [applause]

Q: Mr. LaRouche, my name is D—. The 25th Amendment is to be activated by the cabinet of the United States. Which members, of those would be able to—John Kerry would be one, right? Or no? Who would be the principals of the cabinet who would make this decision?

youtube

Obama's Murders: Mass beheadings of Egyptian Christians being carried out by Islamic State terrorists on the beach in Libya.

Use the 25th Amendment

LaRouche: You had the first precedent with the 25th Amendment. The 25th Amendment resulted in the bouncing out of a President. And the precedent of this action became the 25th Amendment; which means that if there are abuses by an incumbent President of the United States, and he engages in lawless proceedings, then he can be suspended by a proceeding in the body of the United States' ruling forces; as compared to the usual idea of impeaching a President who violates the principles of our nation. And Obama should be thrown out of office immediately, because he has violated the provisions specified under the terms of the 25th Amendment. And that would be a blessing, and not in disguise.

Q: [follow-up] It would be!

Q: Good afternoon, sir. Thank you for everything you do to stop oppression in the world. I am M__ from Mali, my home country. I was born Muslim, and I converted to Christianity. But I have been persecuted for that. That's why I'm here and became a citizen. Now ISIS is killing Christians in Middle East, and forcing Christians to convert to Islam. Do you think something is possible to stop that terror? And what should the Obama Administration do about violence against Christians in the world?

LaRouche: OK, good. Well, first of all, we have the problem right now, Obama. Obama is the number-one problem, because the President of the United States,— if Obama were not the President, shall we say, then that represents the agency for which we can get justice from the kind of problem you are talking about.

Now, also other nations—Europe has got a very poor record right now, in general. Germany has not lived up to its moral standards on this, though many German officials *have* stood for good causes. But there are some ruling forces there who don't want that to happen. We find, for example, the British system; well, the British system is a horrible, evil system. But we have now a new campaign coming up where a new election may occur in the United Kingdom, and they might get rid of this nonsense. So this time, there are various kinds of things which could be successful good things to be done, to deal with these problems.

The main thing is, if we, in the United States, dumped Obama, threw him out of office, under the conditions of the 25th Amendment, then we *ourselves* would be free.

See the problem here is this: Most Americans are cowards. It's not that they were built to be cowards, but they are intimidated. Now if, for example, you take the conditions of economic life in the United States, see what has happened to the standard of living of people in the United States who used to be skilled workers, for example; skilled employees, people with scientific capabilities, and so forth. *We don't have many more of those any more.* The majority of the labor force of the United States is almost crushed. We're losing everything. Our children are becoming insane, and corrupt. It's not necessary, but it was forecast.

So the point is, we do have causes which we in the United States, in concert with people from other nations, can move ahead, and get this thing put in the right

Well, the problem is,—it's a really serious problem here—that we've had two Presidencies, which are actually four Presidencies, of Bush who was re-elected; and of Obama who was re-elected, in the process of completing his second term. All right, now during this period, think about what that means: Who were the children who were born at the time of young Bush's or Obama's Presidency? What has happened in eight years? What has happened to children in eight years, from very young age to adolescence? What are these children fit for? How many of them are fit at all? Under the reign of Bush and Obama?

direction. It doesn't mean an immediate, wonderful miracle, it means moving rapidly in the right direction. And therefore, those of us who are concerned about it just have to do that. Just do it, and we can do it. That is, it's possible for us to do it.

But the problem we have, is basically most Americans today are so intimidated, so poorly educated, so isolated from things that it used to be you could take for granted, and that's not taken for granted any more. And therefore, we have to mobilize what we have as forces in the United States and beyond. We have to make a change in direction. And the kind of thing you're worrying about are the kind of things that come under "change in direction." Without the change in direction, you can't make it. So let's do it. Let's make the change.

Q: Good afternoon, Mr. LaRouche. I'm P__ from Connecticut—I was going to say the "Dodd-Frank State." [laughter] Anyway.

I have two things: One's a question, and one is an idea. I think I'll give you the idea first: With the upcoming General Assembly, the United Nations is an excellent place for a rally. On Wednesday, I plan on bringing five, 3 by 5, full-size flags representing the BRICS nations, to add to our posters and signs. What do you think of this idea?

LaRouche: I think it's perfectly feasible. I don't know if it would be successful, but the idea of doing it, right now, it's feasible. It's something that should be done. I mean, you don't have to get the full answer; you don't have to get the full detail of how it's going to work out. It's a question of attitude. If you're pushing with the right attitude, you probably can come out with some success.

Children of Bush/Obama

Q: [follow-up] Hmm! Thank you.

The second thing was, can we focus on the prosecutors, to impeach Obama?

LaRouche: Yes! That's the 25th Amendment. And

when you get enough members of the Congress, who realize that this bum has to be thrown out of office, quick, that'll do the job. That's what has to happen.

Q: [follow-up] Thank you very much.

Q: Good afternoon, Lyn, this is M__ from New York, and I think it's very, very important that you spoke about education, I think four speakers ago, and then the last couple of speakers you've touched on that as well. Now, obviously, 16-, 17-year-olds, at this point, young men, young women, it's essential for them to participate in their own survival, I think, to put it bluntly. And also, since we are adamant,—and we need to increase this adamancy,—that we will get to the next elections, in other words, the selection of new leadership for this country, hopefully in a drastically different direction, from the direction we've been going in.

My question is, how can we use, I think most significantly, Classical literature, Classical art, Classical music, Classical drama, to imbue these young men and young women with the conceptions both to participate in their own survival; in the process of saving the country, and then, in exercising the leadership that is necessary to progress the United States of America? Thank you, Lyn.

LaRouche: Well, the problem is,—it's a really serious problem here—that we've had two Presidencies, which are actually four Presidencies, of Bush who was re-elected; and of Obama who was re-elected, in the process of completing his second term. All right, now during this period, think about what that means: Who were the children who were born at the time of young Bush's or Obama's Presidency? What has happened in eight years? What has happened to children in eight years, from very young age to adolescence? What are these children fit for? How many of them are fit at all? Under the reign of Bush and Obama?

In other words, therefore, what you have is you have a cowardly citizenry. Why are they cowardly? Because they're afraid of their own children! Their own children

> Now, science is what? Science is the uniqueness which defines the distinction between human beings and animals. What does that mean? That means that mankind develops powers, creative powers in the universe, powers which become the foundations of what we should call science. In other words, mankind's mind is able to create. For example, let's take two cases: Kepler, Kepler who discovered the Solar System. Did he use mathematics? No. He was smart enough not to. He discovered a principle in the universe which no mathematician had ever known.

are various kinds of drunks; they have no orientation to anything that's meaningful in life. And parents of these children are stunned; what can they do, to have created these children? What're we going to do with these children?

And so, therefore we need a very active approach to this matter, and obviously, the thing is culture; culture, as such. Take them aside, convince them that some of the things they were thinking about were kind of kooky, and wrong! And dangerous. Or, the other one is to say, "Where the hell do you think your life is going, the way you're going?" And some young people will respond to that. They'll regret the fact that they were drunks and all kinds of drug addicts; and the sex life, we don't which sex there is in the human species any more. The thing is so damned confused, we don't know who's voting for what, and who's breeding with whom, or what.

So the problem is, we really have to realize, we have to have a revolution in the sense of morals, in the sense of Classical artistic composition, in terms of scientific development; in terms of educating people to think in terms of what their brains can do! And what do they run on? Drugs! Drugs and drug-like access; what comes out of that? They become unfit to live. And why does this happen? Because it's encouraged.

How many people are actually employed among the youth, in the United States today? How many are not? How many may be employed a little bit, but not very much; their skills? Almost nil! Scientific training? Almost nothing! So how do we expect the civilization to function in this way? It means, we face at the best, we're threatened by an emergency, a cultural emergency.

I believe the problem can be solved; but I don't believe it can happen automatically. It has to be solved. And we have to take the best we have in terms of the cultural achievement of our body of citizens, and encourage that, to spread it, and hope that the infection will do the job.

Q: [follow-up] Thank you very much, Lyn. [applause]

Mathematics Versus Science

Q: Hello, Mr. LaRouche. My name is G__ from here in Manhattan. I have taught mathematics for over 50 years. When I was here last week, I reacted very strongly, when you seemed to attack mathematics. I understand that mathematics is not a science, but a tool for science to use. Nevertheless, don't you think that the teaching of math has a place in the basic curriculum? Thank you very much.

LaRouche: No, not really. What it does have, it has an experience which a child can get, a young child can get, or adolescent. And they can reach a certain kind of discipline. But the minute you get them into the process of competent discipline, which is the so-called mathematics routine, it doesn't really work for science. Therefore, you have to understand the difference between mathematics and science; and science is based on the discovery of new principles, or the equivalent of new principles which overthrow—for example, my education is based on Bernhard Riemann. I'm a Riemannian product; and Riemann was not a mathematician: He said *Don't* do this! it's a mistake! And I say: Don't do it, it's a mistake!

But even to acquaint the young students, to acquaint them with what mathematics is, then you have to take the next step; say, "now we told you about mathematics. Now we'll tell you what's wrong about it." And Bernhard Riemann will make the point very clearly!

Q: [follow-up] Well, sir, I'm not sure I agree with all of that. but nevertheless, I thank you for your opinion.

Q: Hi, Mr. LaRouche. I'm R__ from Bergen County, New Jersey. My question involves recent events in the economics sphere. I want to quote, basically paraphrase you from the website. "LaRouche: The trans-Atlantic System Is Over, Replace It Now." And I thought there was a very succinct and to the point paragraph in there, which I'd like to read, quickly:

"LaRouche ridiculed the idea that the so-called 'Black Monday' stock market meltdown of Aug. 24 was the cause of the crisis; the crash was only a display of the fact that the markets are starting to catch up with the reality of the system's total bankruptcy. It is also wrong to blame China for the crisis. They have been put through the wringer, because of the global trade collapse which affects their economy significantly, but they are *not* the cause, LaRouche emphasized."

I really like that paragraph, because it very succinctly summarizes the concerns that I have in reading the common media. And you can see quite clearly in the media that the blame is trying to be put on China as the source of this crisis: "Oh, it's because of the Chinese. Why? Because the Chinese are having problems, and they're not buying stuff any more so the commodities countries are having severe problems, and they're going to have to go off their currency pegs and that's going to cause a meltdown. But the United States is fine."

That seems to be the attitude in the media: There's nothing wrong with the United States; the United States is always good, always has been good, always will be good, and there's nothing conceivably wrong with the U.S. economy. That seems to be the attitude you get in the press.

Well, you can get a glimmer here and there, "well, maybe the growth isn't as good as it should be, or could be." So over the past week, I was thinking about economic growth; what causes economic growth. Nobody in the media seems to have an answer to that. You read the *Wall Street Journal*, you get platitudes of "It's caused by, well, we need technology in order to grow the economy," but they don't really go any further than that. And one writer actually says, "We need more deregulation." [LaRouche laughs] So the way to grow to the economy, to some people, is to deregulate everything, that'll somehow, by magic...

Now, in thinking about these issues, I was thinking about the idea of energy-flux density, which I know you pioneered that concept; and I came to the conclusion that you can't have serious economic growth without— as I understand it, you state it this way; you say, economic growth can be measured by the increase in the productive capacity of workers, and I think one could hook that up with increasing energy-flux density. Because if the technology platform is at a higher level, then for the same human effort you're going to get increased output.

So I see the concept of energy-flux density as crucial of the increase in energy-flux density of the kind that can only be attained through fusion power, as being essential to talking seriously about increasing the economic growth. Do you have any comments on that?

The Task of Mankind

LaRouche: Yes. I can actually make a clarification of what this whole thing of mathematics and science is. And what's the difference between mathematics and science. Mathematics is not science; it has a role which is in a life of science, but it is not science. In other words, for example, a student makes a calculation based on mathematics, and the student will find out in due course, that that doesn't work. Now, the fact that the student had studied the fact, and now finds out that it was wrong, that it doesn't work, then the student has to go to the next step, to science. Get out of mathematics and go into science.

Now, science is what? Science is the uniqueness which defines the distinction between human beings and animals. What does that mean? That means that mankind develops powers, creative powers in the universe, powers which become the foundations of what we should call science. In other words, mankind's mind is able to create. For example, let's take two cases: Kepler, Kepler who discovered the Solar System. Did he use mathematics? No. He was smart enough not to. He discovered a principle in the universe which no mathematician had ever known.

The same thing has happened recently in terms of the system of water. The human stock of water supply is located not only on Earth in the main; it's mainly in the Galaxy. That is, the sources of water used by mankind depend ultimately on the superior volume of that process, from the Galaxy.

So therefore, what happens is the history of mankind, including the biological discoveries of science, which are not mathematical, so therefore, you cannot rely on mathematics for anything except pedestrian purposes. For scientific purposes, mathematics is not relevant. And I think Kepler, for example, would understand that, and he demonstrated it. Einstein understood it; Einstein was the only man who understood science, adequately, during the Twentieth Century.

So the task of mankind is to make scientific progress, to enable mankind to create achievements in production, which no animal could ever have done! Sometimes animals and poorly educated people, can make discoveries; but they're not scientific discoveries. And therefore, the point is we have to make discoveries; we are going to have to deal with the Galaxy. Our water supply for mankind on Earth depends upon the Galactic process; we now have discovered some facts about that Galactic process in recent times, and it's that Galactic process, which will ultimately guarantee the ability of mankind to maintain human life on planet Earth.

So *these* are the conditions. You have to rely on actual science! Mathematics *will not do it*, it has to be science. Not mathematics. And therefore, yes, we can do things with mathematics, we can take existing technologies, use existing technologies in new ways. That's done, that's legitimate. But it's not enough. We need to make fundamental discoveries of universal principle. And that's what's required.

Q: Hello, Mr. LaRouche, H__ from the Bronx. I enjoy these conversations with you. I happen to be personally associated with people from South America, from Central America, from Guatemala, and there have been very bad things happening in Guatemala, due to an operation of Obama and Biden, where ironically they are running an impeachment against the President of Guatemala through an international UN judicial organization, which they forced on the government of Guatemala over the last 10 years.

And then, at the same time, we feel this hate in the U.S. as typified by Mr. Trump against immigrants, against Mexicans, against Guatemalans; it's reminiscent of the Nazi attitudes of the '30s, and I hope somehow we can use this experience to help impeach Obama. But you know, it is getting very dirty, and some of the people I speak to from Central America are actually in quite a bit of fear of this process that we're seeing. So

White House/Pete Souza

Barack Obama confers with Japanese Prime Minister Shinzo Abe before the APEC summit on Nov. 11, 2014.

sort of burning at us.

The Japan Mess

LaRouche: Trump is a fraud. He really is nothing; he has no intellectual notability; he tends to steal a little bit, or a great bit. But he's not really worth talking about, except to say bad things about him. If you want to say bad things about Trump, do it all day! Enjoy yourself.

Q: Hi Lyn, this is D__ in New York: On the subject of creating an effective movement for the 25th Amendment to be implemented, I thought I would share a little bit of an experience I was able to have recently, where I was fortunate enough to visit Japan, for a short amount of time, and I was very inspired by many of the people I met there; I really enjoyed the country. But there's certainly a huge challenge in Japan, namely that the right-wingers in the government are in charge currently of the Prime Ministership in the form of Shinzo Abe, who, for people who aren't aware of this, has recently been in the process of forcing through a reinterpretation of the

I'd like your comments.

LaRouche: Yeah, we have some judges in the United States who are part of this problem of incentives against people of South America and Central America, and those forces inside the United States, who are judges, major judges, and they are part of the gang of a bunch of gangsters who are trying to rape South American nations and Central American nations. So there is a problem, and the problem must find justification.

Q: [follow-up] Yeah, also, if you'd like to comment, this thing about Trump. We thought it would go away, but apparently the cancer is not going away: we had this thing with Trump having a fit against this fellow George Ramos of the Univision organization. And I don't know if you have any special recipe or remedy for this, but it is something that is

Peace Constitution that followed MacArthur's role in the occupation of Japan. And this is a Constitution that prevents Japan from being engaged in war, essentially.

So this is being changed right now. What I was happy to experience was, I was able to attend a rally of some people in Tokyo who stood outside of the Diet, and they were out there to defend the Peace Constitution from Abe. And I was happy to see, also, that in large part, they did not really talk about the critical issue being thermonuclear war and Obama's role, there was some discussion of that; and there was a serious understanding of what Abe represents, who many people don't realize is the grandson of a leading war criminal in fascist Japan, named Kishi. There were some people at this event who had pictures of Abe with a Hitler moustache, much like what you did to Obama.

But I was happy to see that what this movement has been creating over the past few months, and it's galvanizing a number of people who are simply average middle-class people, many of whom are boomer age, who in the 1960s and '70s were engaged in certain protest activities in Japan, and they're building now, for tomorrow, what they intend to be a million people across Japan to protest the reinterpretation of the Peace Constitution. And before I left, I saw one of the posters advertising this, and it had Obama's face behind Abe. So there's a growing understanding of Obama's role.

But it occurs to me,—it's just shocking how over years, people are trying to address the breakdown of this country in terms of this issue or that issue, when the only issue is the Presidency of the United States and Wall Street: Namely, getting rid of Obama, and putting through Glass-Steagall. So somehow in Japan, there's been over this period, amongst these people, many of whom are not political otherwise, but have become political, they have the humility to admit what has been done in their own country, even going back to World War II; because you know, Abe's one of these people who refuses to address the reality of the crimes committed.

So these people have had the humility to try to organize themselves to have the self-confidence to stand up. And my major question at this moment is: we're in a tragedy here in the United States, we're in a tragedy globally, so what is that principle? Is it humility? What is it that is the pathway to the self-confidence that Americans need to organize for the 25th Amendment?

LaRouche: Well, it's more complicated; it looks simple on the stage, but it's not really that clear. Look, guess where Abe came from on this operation? From the United States! This movement in Japan was provoked to attack China. And what was done was part of Obama's pressure to support Abe, and to bring a conflict between China and Japan into play. So we shouldn't look at things on the surface, when we know that—or should know or could know, what's going on.

People in Japan have gone through a lot of things, some of which I know about. I had a very close relationship in the later period, after MacArthur's operation, in terms of working with Japan. And I was working in that part of the world. I was organizing with a Japanese organization, which was a great organization, actually, and made great achievements. And the people who represented that organization were sort of dissipated from their changed conditions.

So the thing you have to do, don't assume that the people who are the active persons on the case, are the force at play. In this case, it is *Obama* who's responsible. You take the emergence of Abe in this new form, is a result of *Obama!* So, you want to solve the problem? Get Obama out!

The Standard of Einstein

Q: Good afternoon, Mr. LaRouche. This question is more intellectual than political, but: Do you think that the fact that Obama's mother was in the State Department, affected his attitude toward the British Crown?

LaRouche: It did, of course. You have to look at this, also, his stepfather, Obama's stepfather: he was the guy who was a real murderous guy. And obviously, the mother was not murderous; the mother was a little bit freaky, kooky, but she was not murderous as such. Obama got it from his stepfather, who was a *real* killer in that part of the world, and that's where the problem came from.

So Obama is evil. But his stepfather is the guy who trained him. And that's where the problem came from.

Q: This is E__ originally from the Bronx, and I have a statement and then a question. Statement: Albert Einstein had a formula that the energy of the universe is constant, so my question to you is, could you elaborate on your concept of negentropy in the universe?

LaRouche: It's the same thing. Of course, the universe is never silent, it's never fixed. In everything we know about it, it's never been fixed. As a matter of fact, the interesting thing about it, when you look at the experience of mankind in science, in developing science, is that mankind is always inherently capable of making discoveries, *new* discoveries, and when you're talking about science, you have to be talking about *new* discovery; *new* principles of discovery.

You cannot use a deductive approach to understand science. You know Albert Einstein himself was exemplary in the fact that that was his method. And all the other official scientists during the Twentieth Century, failed to meet the standard of Einstein, because they accepted mathematics, instead of science. And what happened is, was that at the beginning of the Twentieth Century there was a change in the intellectual life: In the Nineteenth Century, good science was based on discovery of new principles, *not* on mathematics.

Bertrand Russell at the beginning of the Twentieth Century, introduced in force the brainwashing of most of the scientists in the United States and other places; they were brainwashed, and they believed in mathematics, not physical science.

So therefore, the problem has been that those of us who were working on these kinds of issues, have to deal with that problem. Einstein was right, and those who disagreed with Einstein were wrong. Einstein was right, it is the people who turned against him who were wrong. And that's true today.

Any idea of science as science exists today in practice, not as taught by people; much of the education is wrong on this case. The basis for progress is what Einstein represented: *creativity*. Creating a new Solar System in the universe which had never existed before! So you cannot deduce science from mathematics. Because science deals with the things that were not created beforehand.

So the problem is the lack of the effort to provide people, including scientists, with a competent approach to understand what scientific method really means. And that's what we have to fight for: True scientific method, the discovery of universal principles in the Solar System and beyond, principles which had not been known before, but were called into creation at a later point. And the whole history of science all the way back, has already been the discovery of things that mankind had never understood before, as principles. And that's what we have to do.

Q: Good afternoon, Mr. LaRouche. My name is Mr. H___; I've lived since 1959 in Queens, almost, except for my military service time. Now, I have a lot of questions: Power of corporations,—they control our government. Indirectly they control all of us! I believe we live in a rich man's dictatorship, the corporation. How can you break them? They control the newspapers, they control our propaganda, they control our way of thinking. Can we come up with another Dr. Martin Luther King? Can we come up with another Mahatma Gandhi,

---

Any idea of science as science exists today in practice, not as taught by people; much of the education is wrong on this case. The basis for progress is what Einstein represented: creativity. Creating a new Solar System in the universe which had never existed before! So you cannot deduce science from mathematics. Because science deals with the things that were not created beforehand.

---

and change our way of life? There is no more middle class. How much more can we stretch our dollar bill? Look, 11 million Americans lost their homes not long ago: nobody went to jail, but the rich got mortgages! How much more do they want?

The Practical Man Can't Understand Science

LaRouche: Well the problem is, [crosstalk] you have to look at the problem correctly. The point is that most of our society is ignorant, by its own standards: That is, it is not progressive, it is not scientific! That is, it does not make new discoveries of principle, which can be converted to produce results which mankind had never known before. And that's where the problem lies.

Now, if you take a population and they believe that mathematics is science, then you have people who are not, really, good scientists, will never be good scientists under those conditions. And so therefore, the problem here is, again, the Einstein problem: Einstein was the only person present in his generation, *who understood what science is*. The only one! There were other people who had aspects of science, and they were serious; you have people who are still making discoveries which are actually scientific discoveries. But in general in the universities today, there is no understanding of science *per se*; there is an understanding of a mathematical interpretation of what is called science. That's the problem.

However, in the history of the earlier period, like before the Twentieth Century, yeah, there was very good frequent science, real science. Today we're trying to get it born again. And it can be done; it has to be done. And the work with Kepler,—for example, the

Hubble Heritage Team/NASA

The Sombrero Galaxy, as seen from the Hubble telescope on July 26, 2015.

people who have studied Kepler actually understood what Kepler did when he discovered the Solar System. And now we have what was discovered at a higher level, as the Galactic System: these are things that were *unknown*, beforehand. There were not sciences before then of this nature; these were things that had remained unknown. But it's going into the unknown, beyond the unknown, which is the nature of science.

And only mankind can do that. The practical man cannot understand science; only a scientist can understand science, because, why? Because they are making discoveries, and know how to prove new discoveries, as Einstein did. And Einstein was the only person in that century, who really had a legitimate claim to being a scientist; because he was a discoverer.

Q: [follow-up] So, our school system, how are we going to bring it up? How can we compete against the Chinese, against the Europeans? We are being left behind! How can we compete against the world, because I feel we are being left behind compared to the Europeans, even the Chinese; our school system is not the way it has been in the past.

LaRouche: That's true: Your complaint on that account is absolutely correct. However, there are some people who are trying to teach, and who are doing a competent job at what they're trying to teach.

Q: [follow-up] Our children will not have the same—my grandchildren will not have the same opportunity any more...

LaRouche: I know that. But I wouldn't quarrel with

you about that at all. I know what's happened to education; I know how few educators there are still around, who really have a clear head and know how to use it. That's true.

But the problem is, the culture of the United States, since Franklin Roosevelt died, has generally gone in a direction of down! What your complaint is, should be addressed to what destroyed what had been achieved by Franklin Roosevelt. What he represented, and other scientists at the same time, in the same period. Yes! The United States was a great power, and Franklin Roosevelt epitomized the principle of that great power of the United States. Other people who served after him, like some great warriors we had, were not poor at all; we had some great scientists also during that period.

But what happened is the process, like the various clowns, like the FBI and so forth, these clowns did everything possible; if you know what I know, directly, from my age, coming back from military service back into the United States, and what I saw when I got back into the United States and walked back home into the United States; when I began finding out quickly, in a very short time, how evil and corrupt the United States had become.

What is True Immortality?

And I reflected on that, because I had a close relationship with people tied to our President, and what happened was, that they were just almost destroyed; it was crushed. You have to understand—I don't know quite how old you are—but I can tell you what I know, what was done to the people of the United States under the new Presidency after Roosevelt,—it was *ugly* and *evil*. And a lot of that is—I mean, the killing of Kennedy, and the killing of his brother! It was murder! And I know some of the people who did the murder. What was wrong: I was very closely associated with Ronald Reagan. I served him in a special case, a special opera-

Yeah, we're all going to die. Even me, I'm going to die, eventually. I don't know how long I can stick this thing out, but I'm very active at it right now, still. So the issue is, the purpose of mankind is not only to live, but to produce something new for all mankind in one degree or another. And that's what makes the meaning of our existence, immortal. We cannot be immortal; the meaning of our existence by creative forces exercised by us, is immortal. And the thing you want to do with life, is you want to become immortal; that doesn't mean you're going to live forever. It means that you're going to be something which cannot be forgotten.

tion, and I know what they did to him: they shot him! It was a part of the Bush family.

He survived that. And I got the next treatment, next. They didn't actually try to shoot me, but they tried everything else. And so, the Bush family, you tell me about Bush? You tell me about Obama? I can tell you, these things are things that should not have existed, ever.

Q: [follow-up] OK, thank you. Thank you.

Q: [Lynne Speed] Hi Lyn. So I have a question for you about the issue of immortality. And I've been thinking quite a bit about this, this week, because of course, we lost a very, very dear old friend: Amelia Boynton Robinson. She passed away this past Tuesday, after a very, very long, very, very fruitful and productive life; we're not sure whether she was 104 or 110, since I have a copy of her driver's license and passport that says she was born on Aug. 18, 1905.

But at any rate, as you well know, and as many of our people in our Manhattan Project know, she worked since she was a very little girl, starting in the nineteen-teens, registering with her mother people to vote; and she continued right through bringing Martin Luther King into Selma, Alabama into the whole voting rights fight, and so on. And then, even after all of that, at the ripe old age, of who knows? 70, then, she joined with you and with Helga and served as the Vice-Chairwoman of the Schiller Institute for 25 years, bringing her message for the uplifting of humanity to the entire world. So it is a great loss.

But you have spoken many times, recently, about this question of immortality: that one's life is not simply the measure of what we do it in, great as the things that we might accomplish are, but what we leave for future posterity. And I would like you to comment on this, at this point in terms of this question of immortality.

LaRouche: Immortality, I would say, is expressed by true scientific creativity. Mathematics is not cre-

ative, intrinsically. Mathematics is useful, but it depends upon the prediscovery of an advanced principle, and then once you have discovered the advanced principle, then that principle becomes an addition which you may call mathematical. But the reason it's called mathematical, is because science has changed mathematics. And it's taken and brought mathematics to a higher level of science.

Without this progress of science, going beyond mathematics, going into science as such, making discoveries which are actually scientific discoveries, what's that mean?

And we are each born, and we die. What's the meaning of all that? The meaning is, yes, we're all going to die. We'll die eventually anyway; we're not immortal. But mankind is immortal. Because mankind, by the progress of mankind in making the effect of scientific progress, scientific discovery, not mathematical, *scientific* discoveries, these things are the secret of mankind's access to immortality as a species. And that's what's important.

Yeah, we're all going to die. Even me, I'm going to die, eventually. I don't know how long I can stick this thing out, but I'm very active at it right now, still. So the issue is, the purpose of mankind is not only to live, but to produce something new *for all mankind* in one degree or another. And that's what makes the meaning of our existence, immortal. We cannot be immortal; the meaning of our existence by creative forces exercised by us, is immortal. And the thing you want to do with life, is you want to become immortal; that doesn't mean you're going to live forever. It means that you're going to be something which cannot be forgotten. [applause]

Mankind Must Take Charge

SPEED: We've come to the end, again, and there's something in particular I think we can do. As you know, Lyn, we had a rally this Wednesday at Wall Street.

We're going to go back this week. When we sign off from you, we're going to be teaching some people one of our Wall Street songs in anticipation of that.

But I'd like to point something out which is well-known to you, but may not be so well-known to people here: You know, there've been a lot of people we've been associated with. There were people like Hulan Jack, the Borough President of Manhattan, and he suffered tremendously. There was Fred Wills, and he was the former Foreign Minister of Guyana and Justice Minister, and he suffered tremendously. And there was of course, Amelia. There was Wade Watts, your friend Wade Watts, who was the head of the Oklahoma NAACP, and had converted the Grand Dragon of the Ku Klux Klan to Christianity [laughter], and you know, Wade suffered all the time! Of course, he was a gambler before he became a preacher, and did many things.

You have attracted a rogues' gallery of heroic people, over the years. And of course, the whole purpose I see of the Manhattan Project, is, we are in the practice of producing such rogues, if you want to put it that way: In other words, real Americans. Real people who really know how to fight. You've talked about this idea: Wall Street goes now, and we're going to be taking

that up, as soon as this signs off.

So I'd like you, if you want to, tell us how you'd like us to proceed with that in the coming week.

LaRouche: [laughs] Well, we have a couple of miracles to make first of all: We have to push urgently, we have to push through getting rid of Obama. Get him out of office. Because if we don't get him out of office, he is already committed to launch a thermonuclear war. That's what he's working for. He's been shifting everything in his administration to clear the way for launching a thermonuclear war. And a thermonuclear war, if you want to understand what it is, means that practically nobody survives. Not under a thermonuclear war. The best plan they've got there, is maybe 1 million people will survive. That's what the issue is.

And therefore, mankind has to take charge and get the Obama syndrome out of office. And in one way or the other, the 25th Amendment to the Constitution is the instrument that should be allowed, to get Obama out of office. That would prevent World War III. And it's a pretty good idea! [applause]

SPEED: So that concludes our dialogue with Lyn for this week, and we will, of course, see you next week, Lyn!

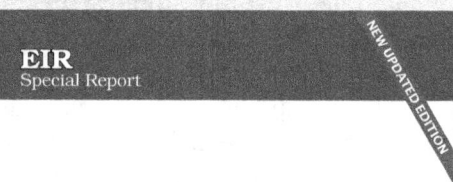

Pre-empt! FDR's First Hundred Days

by Michael Steger

"At such periods there is an accumulation of the power of communicating and receiving intense and impassioned conceptions respecting man and nature."

—Percy Bysshe Shelley
A Defence of Poetry, 1821

Franklin Roosevelt's First Hundred Days was not a bureaucratic playbook, neither was it simply the result of effective management and political deal-making, and if it were to be reduced to such, it would add little benefit to solving our nation's immediate crisis. The essence of FDR's First Hundred Days as President was driven by nothing less than a poetic and creative impulse to act, as FDR is often quoted from his first inaugural address: "The Nation asks for action, and action now." Not simply for the immediate restoration of the nation's physical survival, which it certainly accomplished, but, to greater effect, ending the cultural deterioration and rampant degeneracy of the nation's leadership, as well as the nation's culture generally—a degeneration which had increasingly accelerated since the assassination of President William McKinley in 1901.

These first hundred days, beginning from March 4th with his first Inaugural address and the implementation of the Emergency Banking Act, to June 16, 1933 and the passage of the Glass-Steagall Banking Act, was nothing less than a compositional lunge, conceived by conviction in the years prior to his actual inauguration, and intending to accomplish nothing less than the revival of the nation to the heritage of Lincoln and Grant before him, i.e. to fully restore the power of the nation to the legacy of Alexander Hamilton, with the added strength of major scientific and artistic advancements since the Civil War, and finally and for good, end the international power of the Wall Street slave system otherwise known as the British Empire.

It should be obvious, but requires emphasis under the current strains of national cowardice, that had FDR's powers not been cut short by his untimely death, and had his personal mission been carried on by more than just the few patriotic Americans of a similar elevated dedication, we would not face the threat of imminent financial disintegration and nuclear war today.

Following FDR's death, the nation faced an immedi-

National Archives

FDR on the eve of his first Fireside Chat, March 12, 1933, where he presented the Emergency Banking Act.

ate return to the process of cultural deterioration which he so adamantly had opposed. Under such regression, we now unnecessarily endure the psychotic, mass-murderous administration of Obama—the epitome of our degeneration—and his unceasing threats of nuclear war against, and not coincidentally, two of FDR's greatest allies in World War II, Russia and China. Where are the great Americans?

What must and can be launched in the coming weeks, if not days ahead, is an immediate revival of FDR's creative spirit—a shared commitment to eliminate the plague of Wall Street, and as Lyndon LaRouche recently expressed, "bury the dead,"—reviving the creative and productive spirit of genius that currently lies dormant in the good people of our nation. It was FDR and his close set of advisers, who, while facing massive opposition from fascists foreign and domestic, unleashed the creative potential of our nation beginning with the First Hundred Days.

Today, under new and better leadership, and with allies counting more than half the world's seven billion souls, we shall consolidate this potential and fulfill FDR's ardent wish on a global scale. This must not wait until January of 2017; it must begin now. Labor day weekend will suffice.

Shut Down Wall Street

Even prior to day one as President, FDR was ruthless with Wall Street, both with the men and their culture. Following FDR's election, then-Assistant District Attorney for Manhattan Ferdinand Pecora was appointed as the third and final chief counsel to a special Senate investigation of the corrupt banking practices which led to the 1929 crash. Pecora proceeded to expose the systemic criminal fraud of Wall Street by investigating the leading culprits: Charles Mitchell, President of National City Bank—then the largest bank in the nation,

Library of Congress

John Pierpont Morgan, Jr.—Wall Street banker and funder of Mussolini.

and who was actually arrested and indicted; J.P. Morgan, Jr. of J.P. Morgan and Co.; and Richard Whitney, President of the New York Stock Exchange. The stage was being set for FDR's nationwide and revolutionary return to a Hamiltonian banking system after his inauguration.

Yet, just three weeks prior to his inauguration, FDR was nearly killed by an assassination attempt in Miami,—and then, one week later, a nationwide bank panic was instigated, forcing most of the banks throughout the country to close for lack of funds. Together, these constituted a blatant attempt to disrupt FDR's Presidency,—equivalent to the planned assassination of Abraham Lincoln on a train through Baltimore to his inauguration in Washington, combined with the planned attack on Ft. Sumter.

FDR took immediate emergency measures, equating the now-escalated crisis to a wartime environment in his inaugural address, and identifying Wall Street financiers and speculators—who were no different from the fascists in Europe—as the known aggressors and enemies to be defeated.[1]

Looking back at this process as it had unfolded four years earlier, he said in 1936, as he again accepted the Democratic nomination:

> These economic royalists complain that we seek to overthrow the institutions of America. What they really complain of is that we seek to take away their power. Our allegiance to American institutions requires the overthrow of this kind of power. In vain they seek to hide behind the flag and the Constitution. In their blindness they forget what the flag and the Constitution stand

---

1. It is well known that J.P. Morgan, Jr. provided direct loans to Mussolini, while Prescott Bush of the Harriman banking interests, the father of President George H.W. Bush, provided loans to Hitler.

for. Now, as always, they stand for democracy, not tyranny; for freedom, not subjection; and against a dictatorship by mob rule and the over privileged alike.

Back in 1933, at his first inauguration, he had addressed this same treason in the broader cultural framework which he intended to transform, by inciting the optimism and imagination of the American people:

Plenty is at our doorstep, but a generous use of it languishes in the very sight of the supply. Primarily this is because the rulers of the exchange of mankind's goods have failed, through their own stubbornness and their own incompetence, have admitted their failure, and abdicated. Practices of the unscrupulous money changers stand indicted in the court of public opinion, rejected by the hearts and minds of men.

True they have tried, but their efforts have been cast in the pattern of an outworn tradition. Faced by failure of credit they have proposed only the lending of more money. Stripped of the lure of profit by which to induce our people to follow their false leadership, they have resorted to exhortations, pleading tearfully for restored confidence. They know only the rules of a generation of self-seekers. They have no vision, and when there is no vision the people perish.

The money changers have fled from their high seats in the temple of our civilization. We may now restore that temple to the ancient truths. The measure of the restoration lies in the extent to which we apply social values more noble than mere monetary profit.

Happiness lies not in the mere possession of money; it lies in the joy of achievement, in the thrill of creative effort. The joy and moral stimu-

---

The Revival of Hamilton's Manhattan Project, Then and Today

FDR, a devout family historian, knew well his own ancestor Isaac Roosevelt's relationship to Hamilton, and not only personally defended Hamilton in his senior thesis at Harvard, but went so far as to attack the clear and malicious attempt by Wall Street to spread the slave-based Confederacy throughout the nation.[1]

He wrote in his Harvard thesis, in 1901 no less, the year of McKinley's assassination:

Washington, the first President under the Constitution, made Hamilton Secretary of the Treasury—the greatest of the Cabinet offices. As he had stabilized the problems of State, so now he ordered the finances of the country and it was his impetus that removed for all time the risk of disintegration of the states.

None appreciated this solidarity more than Aaron Burr, who, defeated for the Presidency in his race against Jefferson, largely through the efforts of Hamilton, saw in this greater financial security the banishment of his dream of establishing a Northern Confederacy.

FDR then followed in Hamilton's footsteps, dropping out of Columbia College early to begin his political involvement in rescuing the nation's economic and cultural life.

So it should come as no surprise that Roosevelt's close set of collaborators, as well as his leading political operatives, were part of Hamilton's Manhattan, sharing a commitment with Roosevelt from the very beginning of his political life, and as he went on to be Governor of New York, and throughout his Presidency.

Eleanor Roosevelt, Harry Hopkins, Frances Perkins, Louis Howe, and Ferdinand Pecora are only a few of the well-known New Yorkers who collaborated with FDR on reviving the true United States from the chains of Wall Street's Confederacy.

And so it is again today from Hamilton's Manhattan, now with the LaRouche Political Movement, that we shape the soon-to-be-incoming Presidency towards a new FDR-inspired recovery.

---

1. See Ingraham, Robert D., "Manhattan's Struggle for Human Freedom Against the Slave Power of Virginia," *EIR*, May 8, 2015.

lation of work no longer must be forgotten in the mad chase of evanescent profits. These dark days will be worth all they cost us if they teach us that our true destiny is not to be ministered unto but to minister to ourselves and to our fellow men.

Recognition of the falsity of material wealth as the standard of success goes hand in hand with the abandonment of the false belief that public office and high political position are to be valued only by the standards of pride of place and personal profit; and there must be an end to a conduct in banking and in business which too often has given to a sacred trust the likeness of callous and selfish wrongdoing. Small wonder that confidence languishes, for it thrives only on honesty, on honor, on the sacredness of obligations, on faithful protection, on unselfish performance; without them it cannot live.

Restoration calls, however, not for changes in ethics alone. This Nation asks for action, and action now.

And action he took. With the Emergency Banking Act of 1933 (EBA), implemented over a bank holiday that started thirty-six hours after his inauguration and lasted for one week, FDR took executive control over the nation's banking system, and investments were soon restarted to critical areas of employment, agriculture, and power development. The EBA was the kind of executive leadership that Hamilton and the founders of our Constitution knew was necessary under such duress. FDR, with his vision of long-term development, immediately ended Wall Street's control of the nation's financial system, and restored such confidence that as soon as the banking holiday had ended, deposits increased.

The Glass-Steagall Act, which was enacted three months later in June, was the *coup de grace* to Wall Street's dominance over the U.S. banking system, and impeded Wall Street's ability to dominate the commercial aspect of U.S. banking for the next sixty-six years until its final repeal in 1999. Its restoration today would be nothing less than a short dirge for Wall Street, since the insane proportions to which they have leveraged the commercial assets of the current banking system into criminal speculation, far exceed, by orders of magnitude, the level of criminal fraud of the 1920s. Providing Wall Street an appropriate cheap burial, it would then liberate the productive powers of labor of our nation with full-throated potential, freed from the burden of such Satanic speculative gambling.

Through these two acts combined,—first, the intervention through the Treasury over the banking system to restore national confidence immediately, and then, the prescient Glass-Steagall bill which restored for generations Hamilton's General Welfare principle of the Constitution,—we have the most efficient and critical means available today, to prevent the total bankruptcy of the U.S. economy, and restore investments into criti-

---

Roosevelt's Emergency Banking Act of 1933

Here are relevant sections of that March 1933 emergency banking legislation:

"During such emergency period as the President of the United States by proclamation may prescribe, no member bank of the Federal Reserve System shall transact any banking business except to such extent and subject to such regulations, limitations and restrictions as may be prescribed by the Secretary of the Treasury, with the approval of the President....

"Whenever he shall deem it necessary in order to conserve the assets of any bank for the benefit of the depositors and other creditors thereof, the Comptroller of the Currency may appoint a conservator for such bank and require of him such bond and security as the Comptroller of the Currency deems proper....

"The conservator, under the direction of the Comptroller, shall take possession of the books, records, and assets of every description of such bank, and take such action as may be necessary to conserve the assets of such bank pending further disposition of its business as provided by law....

"The Comptroller of the Currency is hereby authorized and empowered, with the approval of the Secretary of the Treasury, to prescribe such rules and regulations as he may deem necessary in order to carry out the provisions of this title."

cal areas of employment and development. As we now witness the ongoing disintegration of the Wall Street trans-Atlantic system, anything less than these actions will immediately endanger the economic and spiritual welfare of our nation.

Increase the Productive Powers of Labor

FDR entered office knowing we needed to restore the confidence of the American people, not simply to stop the panic, but most important, to re-engage the people of the nation in the process of self-development as well as of self-government. He addresses both concerns directly to the American people in his second fireside chat of May 7, 1933:

On self-government:

National Archives

Irrigation works being constructed by the Civilian Conservation Corps in Idaho in 1941.

The Congress, and when I say Congress I mean the members of both political parties, fully understood this and gave me generous and intelligent support. The members of Congress realized that the methods of normal times had to be replaced in the emergency by measures which were suited to the serious and pressing requirements of the moment. There was no actual surrender of power, Congress still retained its constitutional authority and no one has the slightest desire to change the balance of these powers. The function of Congress is to decide what has to be done and to select the appropriate agency to carry out its will. This policy it has strictly adhered to. The only thing that has been happening has been to designate the President as the agency to carry out certain of the purposes of the Congress. This was constitutional and in keeping with the past American tradition.

On the immediate restoration of the powers of self-development:

First, we are giving opportunity of employment to one-quarter of a million of the unemployed, especially the young men who have dependents, to go into the forestry and flood-prevention work. This is a big task because it means feeding, clothing, and caring for nearly twice as many men as we have in the regular army itself. In creating this civilian conservation corps we are killing two birds with one stone. We are clearly enhancing the value of our natural resources and second, we are relieving an appreciable amount of actual distress. This great group of men have entered upon their work on a purely voluntary basis, no military training is involved and we are conserving not only our natural resources but our human resources. One of the great values to this work is the fact that it is direct and requires the intervention of very little machinery.

Second, I have requested the Congress and have secured action upon a proposal to put the great properties owned by our Government at Muscle Shoals to work after long years of wasteful inaction, and with this a broad plan for the improvement of a vast area in the Tennessee Valley. It will add to the comfort and happiness of hundreds of thousands of people and the incident benefits will reach the entire nation.

Next, the Congress is about to pass legislation that will greatly ease the mortgage distress among the farmers and the homeowners of the nation, by providing for the easing of the burden of debt now bearing so heavily upon millions of our people.

Our next step in seeking immediate relief is a grant of half a billion dollars to help the states, counties, and municipalities in their duty to care for those who need direct and immediate relief....

We are planning to ask the Congress for legislation to enable the Government to undertake public works, thus stimulating directly and indirectly the employment of many others in well-considered projects.

Further legislation has been taken up which goes much more fundamentally into our economic problems.... The extent of its use will depend entirely upon what the future has in store.

He also condemned the Confederates who still ran rampant, as they do today, over the Hamiltonian idea of national development:

All of this has been caused in large part by a complete lack of planning and a complete failure to understand the danger signals that have been flying ever since the close of the World War...."

It is wholly wrong to call the measure that we have taken Government control of farming, control of industry, and control of transportation. It is rather a partnership between Government and farming and industry and transportation, not partnership in profits, for the profits would still go to the citizens, but rather a partnership in planning and partnership to see that the plans are carried out.

Let me illustrate with an example. Take the cotton goods industry.... The unfair ten per cent could produce goods so cheaply that the fair ninety per cent would be compelled to meet the unfair conditions. Here is where government comes in. Government ought to have the right and will have the right, after surveying and planning for an industry, to prevent, with the assistance of the overwhelming majority of that industry, unfair practice and to enforce this agreement by the authority of government.

Yet FDR's greatest and most sustained intervention against the Wall Street Confederacy, and what became the most effective as well as most enduring of his many three-letter job programs,—including even the allegor-ical, yet accurate story of Harry Hopkins setting up a card table in a hallway and putting nearly fifteen million people to work,—was the Tennessee Valley Authority. Not only for its statistical and financial success, but because it demonstrates Roosevelt's broader commitment for the physical transformation of the nation's economic and cultural powers of labor. Had he survived beyond the end of the war, similar and even greater projects would have been adopted, as we saw with the revolutionary Manhattan Project during the war, and Eleanor Roosevelt's endorsement of President Kennedy's Apollo Project aspirations, both of which were greatly dependent on the scientific and industrial skills developed by the TVA.

The TVA was initiated as part of the First Hundred Days on May 18, 1933, but, like many of his New Deal projects, including the St. Lawrence Seaway and the Boulder Dam projects,—i.e. three of the "Four Corners" hydro-electric projects,—this was an integral part of his commitment to overturn the cultural and economic decay of the country as early as 1929 while Governor of New York, if not earlier. The success of the TVA is impossible to fully capture in the context of this article, yet it could be argued, and without much difficulty, that it is still, even today, the most successful economic project ever initiated! Transforming an area known even before the Great Depression for its severe poverty, the TVA elevated one of the most backwater areas of the old Confederate system into one of the most productive areas in the world in terms of farming, industry, science, and power supply. There are few nations which have not sent engineers and policy planners to the TVA to measure with their own eyes the miracle of its success.

By 1942, the TVA became home to the second successful nuclear reactor ever built. The Manhattan Project had been integrated into the TVA thanks to the TVA's abundance of power supply and industrial capacity. Later, the Oak Ridge National Laboratory joined it as a national training facility for nuclear engineering. In its essence, the TVA was nothing less than a transformation of the human species, from the backwaters of poor southern subsistence farming to the cutting edge of scientific research, a quintessential model of non-linear universal human development.

FDR had intended as much. Similar points could be made regarding the development of the Boulder Dam and the Grand Coulee Dam for the development of water and power for the west. Only the limitations of

The nation's second nuclear plant, called Brown's Ferry, built by the TVA.

this report prevent further demonstration of FDR's broad vision of the potential of the human species and the role of leadership as the means for success in similar endeavors.

Inspire Creative Genius

It has been brought to the attention of this writer that one of FDR's high school papers presented a defense of the English poet and political thinker Percy Bysshe Shelley, and particularly for his scientific view of the human mind and the Creator alike, against the formalist's accusation of some depraved adherence to atheism. This would not be surprising. It would also be accurate as to Shelley's personal universal outlook. (Harry Hopkins, FDR's closest and most trusted collaborator throughout his Presidency, was also a devoted advocate of both Shelley and Keats.)

It is not possible for an empiricist to grasp the means by which FDR accomplished his First Hundred Days, though the facts certainly stand for themselves as an impressive physical accomplishment. A mathematician would merely see the list of actions, and miss the physical transformation entirely. What FDR accomplished was nothing less than the third American Revolution,—the first led by Washington and Hamilton, and the second by Lincoln and Ulysses S. Grant, each and all

from Manhattan's impregnable stronghold against the slaveholders of Wall Street and the South.

Lyndon LaRouche has emphasized as part of his efforts to create an FDR recovery program, with extra emphasis on new Executive leadership, that such policies stem from the human powers of pre-emption. Pre-emption of Wall Street fascism and the obliteration of the trans-Atlantic financial system with Glass-Steagall. Pre-emption of backwater "green" policies of population-reduction with a galactic approach to natural resources, including new sources of rainfall. Pre-emption of the practical, the mathematical, and the mundane, when the profound and preremptory powers of creative discovery and insight are the most critical for ultimate success.

This, FDR and his close coterie of advisors such as Harry Hopkins and Eleanor Roosevelt, understood, because, important to our overall success as are the elimination of Wall Street, and the investments in necessary large-scale development projects,—yet the inspiration of the powers of human discovery is the most essential effect, and that of greatest duration. In essence, it is both the means and the end.

Rare are the artists, scientists, and political leaders who discover that their own personal mission is nothing less than the overall development of mankind. That their own work, either in music or art, science or statecraft, is, with increasing focus, the inspiration and development of the creative powers of mankind. This elevated compassion is seen in the great final works of Johannes Brahms, written while FDR was a boy,—in the struggle of the classical conductor Wilhelm Furtwängler, who not only resisted the fascist culture in tandem with FDR's Presidency, but continued FDR's fight against the Nazis and Wall Street fascists even after the war, with his remarkable insight into the great works by those such as Beethoven, Schubert, and Brahms,—or in the scientific devotion of Albert Einstein, just three years FDR's senior, against mathematical formalists and worse. This was also the devotion of FDR, one discovered throughout his life. He asked, "What is the meaning of my life?" after falling ill with polio, and overcoming enormous physical challenges before then becoming Governor of New York and then President.

Within the small set of his lifelong advisors, Eleanor especially, this was a driving factor in their success, both in the First Hundred Days and throughout, from the triumph against fascism and the restoration of national development, to their commitment to end Empire, including the intended independence of China, India, and all other colonies, to a new system of global development under the new United Nations and Bretton Woods system.

FDR with one of his closest collaborators, his wife Eleanor.

Thus the failure to fulfill FDR's legacy, and to ensure the ultimate success of his endeavors on a world scale, was not simply due to the betrayal by Harry Truman or the traitors on Wall Street. It was the loss of this higher devotion to which FDR was committed, and it is just this which must be revived. This is the devotion of Lyndon LaRouche, as he describes it, from the day he heard of Roosevelt's untimely death. This must also be the devotion of a new Administration, and must be the mission of our nation and her truest citizens.

In the conclusion of his essay, Shelley captures the quality of the historical moment we now, as FDR then, find ourselves:

> The most unfailing herald, companion, and follower of the awakening of a great people to work a beneficial change in opinion or institution, is poetry. **At such periods there is an accumulation of the power of communicating and receiving intense and impassioned conceptions respecting man and nature.** The persons in whom this power resides may often, as far as regards many portions of their nature, have little apparent correspondence with that spirit of good of which they are the ministers. But even whilst they deny and abjure, they are yet compelled to serve the power which is seated on the throne of their own soul. It is impossible to read the compositions of the most celebrated writers of the present day without being startled with the electric life which burns within their words. They measure the circumference and sound the depths of human nature with a comprehensive and all-penetrating spirit, and they are themselves perhaps the most sincerely astonished at its manifestations; for it is less their spirit than the spirit of the age. Poets are the hierophants of an unapprehended inspiration; the mirrors of the gigantic shadows which futurity casts upon the present; the words which express what they understand not; the trumpets which sing to battle, and feel not what they inspire; the influence which is moved not, but moves. Poets are the unacknowledged legislators of the world.

In Shelley's conclusion one can hear what FDR had heard as he read this familiar passage, confronting, and perhaps a little surprised by, the magnitude of his mission and the powers now available. Will we end the Satanic attack upon our people, and all people—will we empower their bodies as well as their souls, and inspire their creative spirit? Were we to consider the content with which FDR approached the initial launch of his Presidency without a consideration of such devotion, we would be looking at the mere shadows of the powers and principles by which humanity advances. If we are to be successful, we must reach beyond those shadows and demonstrate the uniqueness of the human spirit as a principle of creative action. Hence lies the essence of FDR's First Hundred Days and the revolutionary power of his Presidency.

The World Awakens to The Danger of Annihilation

Jeffrey Steinberg of EIR *gave the following review of the global strategic situation to kick off the Aug. 28 LaRouche PAC webcast, (view entire webcast) in response to the institutional question posed to Lyndon LaRouche. That question reads: "Mr. LaRouche, in your opinion, is a political settlement possible in Syria? And if so, what type of collaboration is required from the United States and from Russia?"*

U.S. Navy/Robert S. Price

U.S. and Ukrainian officials at the kickoff of NATO's Sea Breeze-2015 maneuver in the Black Sea, September 1, 2015.

Well, Mr. LaRouche said obviously there is the possibility of solving this terrible crisis, this war that has been waged against Syria for nearly four years now. And of course, the United States and Russia are pivotal to any kind of solution. In fact, the Russian government—President Putin, Foreign Minister Lavrov—have hosted a number of Middle East leaders in Moscow over the past several days.

For example, you had King Abdullah II of Jordan; you had President el-Sisi of Egypt, who spent three days in Moscow, mostly meeting one on one with President Putin. And they worked a great deal on ideas for how to solve the problem of the Islamic State, and the instability that has not only triggered a crisis throughout the Middle East, but has resulted—along with the crisis in Libya—in waves of refugees seeking survival inside continental Europe; flooding an area that is already in profound economic crisis with a humanitarian crisis of severe proportions.

But as Mr. LaRouche emphasized, any possibility of solving the Middle East crisis, as severe as it is, hinges on three preconditions.

The first is that there is virtually no prospect of any kind of appropriate level of Russian or Russian/American cooperation so long as Barack Obama is in the White House. His animus towards Putin has now reached the point where many people internationally, leading figures within the United States and Western Europe, are openly saying that President Obama is driving towards a confrontation with Russia; overtly provoking a confrontation, whether it be over the issue of NATO eastward expansion, the Ukraine situation—where the Administration in Washington persists in supporting outright neo-Nazis from the Right Sector, from the Azov Brigade and others. And where Obama's persistent commitment to the missile defense deployment, which can no longer be credibly considered to be against Iran, is clearly directed against Russia and portends the possibility of a nuclear first strike. So, all of this grave danger centers around the fact that President Obama remains in office.

Secondly, you've got a global financial disintegration process underway right now, centered in the trans-Atlantic region where Wall Street, the City of London, and all of the major trans-Atlantic financial institutions—the so-called too-big-to-fail banks, the underground banks, the non-bank institutions involved in massive capital flight—are all hopelessly bankrupt. They've built up a mountain of debt, measurable in quadrillions [of dollars]...

The Military Warn

But what I want to focus on is the fact that the war danger is immediate, and has, in the past days, become a matter of widespread, public recognition. While much of the major U.S. media has persisted in lying and covering this up, you've got an extraordinary pattern of blunt statements coming out of some of the leading political leaders of the United States, Western Europe, Eastern Europe, and Russia; demanding emergency measures to avert a thermonuclear war of extinction. Now, this process has been ongoing for a number of months, but has really reached a crescendo in the recent days.

But I want to start by referencing back to a very significant article which appeared earlier this year on April 19. To remind people: it was an op-ed published that day in the *New York Times*, and the co-authors were General James E. Cartwright and General Vladimir Dvorkin. General Cartwright, up until fairly recently, had been the Vice Chairman of the U.S. Joint Chiefs of Staff, and had also previously served as the commander of the U.S. Strategic Command; in other words, in charge of the United States' thermonuclear triad. General Dvorkin was head of intelligence for the Russian Strategic Missile Force. So, in other words, these are two people who, throughout their military careers, were directly involved in the threat of nuclear war; and were actually the individuals responsible for implementing orders from the Presidents of their respective countries, if a war were to begin.

Their article was called, "How To Avert a Nuclear War." And they begin by saying, "We find ourselves in an increasingly risky strategic environment. The Ukrainian crisis has threatened the stability of relations between Russia and the West; including the nuclear dimension." And what they go on to say is that right now, because of the nature of the deployment of massive, overkill arsenals of thermonuclear weapons by the United States and Russia, both countries are operating under a doctrine of "launch on warning." Which means that the moment a nuclear launch is detected by one side against the other, the side coming under attack, or perhaps appearing to come under attack, has a very short window of time to decide whether or not to launch a full-scale massive retaliatory strike. And once that happens, you have nuclear annihilation on this planet. So, this article was an extraordinarily clear, cautionary warning.

And later this year, more recently in the Summer, the same two generals, joined by an international group of leading statesmen under an organization called the Nuclear Zero Commission, issued a more elaborate statement. Again, laying out the danger of the doctrine of launch on warning, calling for negotiations between the United States and Russia, and NATO and Russia, to bring an end to this doctrine, because it threatens a nuclear war of extermination on virtually limited notice, measured in minutes, not hours or days. So that statement stands, and there are many other leading military figures who've been joining in issuing the same kinds of warnings.

'We Are At War...'

In the last week, this process has accelerated tremendously. There was a letter issued by a German organization, called the Free Thinkers Association, that was mailed out just three days ago, to every member of the Bundestag, the German parliament, and what they say, just to give a brief quote:

"The war-threatening situation is escalating. After the wars of aggression against Yugoslavia, Afghanistan, Iraq, Libya, and Syria, war is being prepared against Russia. The encirclement of Russia by military bases, the NATO expansion to the East, the construction of a U.S.-missile defense shield, and Western operations in Ukraine, are part of this confrontation. *We are at war and this war can turn into a total one,* French President François Hollande declared in February of 2015. There is the threat of another world war. If a Russia that is attacked, retaliates, what results from that is what former Assistant Minister Willi Wimmer said in November 2014: 'Nothing will be left behind.'"

So that statement is circulating very widely.

Also this week, Jürgen Todenhöfer, who was a former long-time Christian Democratic Union member of the Bundestag, the German parliament, and who has since become a leading anti-war advocate and investigator—he's written several books, the most recent one involved a visit that he paid to Iraq and Syria, where

CC/Hydro

Jürgen Todenhöfer, a German parliamentarian turned anti-war journalist.

he actually was able to interview some leaders of the Islamic State, and actually lived to tell the story—so he has issued an Open Letter to the war politicians of the world. And he says in this letter:

> Dear Presidents and heads of government,
>
> Through decades of a policy of war and exploitation, you have pushed millions of people in the Middle East and Africa into misery. Because of your policies, refugees have to flee all over the world. One out of every three refugees in Germany comes from Syria, Iraq, and Afghanistan. From Africa comes one out of five refugees. Your wars are also the cause of global terrorism. Instead of 100 international terrorists, like 15 years ago, we are now faced with more than 100,000 terrorists. Your cynical ruthlessness now strikes back at us, like a boomerang.

The letter goes on for quite some time and calls for a mass outpouring of protest against this policy of war.

Also, just in the last 24 hours, Professor Antonino Galloni, a leading Italian economist and strategic thinker, has issued a statement published in *Il Domani d'Italia* in which he warns that if there's no fundamental reorganization of the system, economically and politically, the current financial crisis can lead to thermonuclear war. He says:

> The financial crisis makes the conflict among superpowers more likely. China, Russia, and India want to avoid it, whereas American, British, and trans-national lobbies involving weapons lobbies, parallel intelligence agencies, pro-Israeli

organizations, etc. consider war to be the only option at one point. Thus it will be fundamental whether the U.S.A. will regain control of policy.

And so he said: "We need international agreements." Galloni cites a lengthy interview that was given just this past week to the *National Interest* by former U.S. Secretary of State Henry Kissinger, in which Kissinger comes out unusually strongly, warning about the war danger, and saying that the only viable option is to begin serious negotiations with the Russians. Galloni says: We have a problem with the central banking system. They simply continue printing out money to cover up holes in the financial bubble, and he says, quite practically, because of this crisis financially, we risk a thermonuclear conflict. And he says, "The planet's financial means"—in other words, the bubble instruments— "are 54 times the global GDP." He says, "We need a new Bretton Woods (or something similar)," and that all of the toxic assets must be "sterilized." A very strong statement, but I think the critical point is that he emphasizes that the danger of war is coming primarily from the disintegration of a financial system that is hopelessly bankrupt.

Reducing the Risk

Now, there are some leading voices in the United States. Professor Stephen Cohen, known to be one of the leading Russia experts in the United States, has been engaging for the last number of weeks in a weekly dialogue on a major New York City radio station, with the host John Batchelor; and in the past two weeks, Dr. Cohen has focused

youtube

Stephen Cohen, Professor of Russian Studies and Politics at New York University and Princeton.

very specifically on the growing danger of a nuclear war stemming from the policies coming out of the Obama Administration, for confrontation with Russia.

So, again, Mr. LaRouche emphasized that measures, emergency measures, must be taken.

In Europe, the European Leadership Network, which is a grouping of former foreign ministers, de-

White House/Pete Souza

President Barack Obama, a true candidate for the 25th Amendment. Here he's in Selma, Alabama at the commemoration of Bloody Sunday, on March 7, 2015.

fense ministers, other top political figures now retired, have issued their third report since the spring of this year. They've issued two reports, one in July, and one in August, and this third report is bluntly called "Avoiding War in Europe: How to Reduce the Risk of a Military Encounter between Russia and NATO."

What they say is that they've been cataloging an ever-increasing density of military maneuvers and other actions that put NATO forces and Russian forces in close proximity, with major deployments of weapons systems, and that this now represents a grave danger of an incident triggering a general war. They call for a number of measures, including a reconvening of the NATO-Russia Council, to set up rules of conduct, to avoid an incident turning into the trigger for a general war.

Now, as we know, as we've been emphasizing on this broadcast repeatedly, Friday after Friday, the main cause of this war danger is the policy coming out of the Obama White House. There are others in the Administration who are clearly working *against* this war provocation, including the Joint Chiefs of Staff; including, in certain instances, Secretary of State John Kerry. But the thrust coming out of the Obama White House, is for war, and while the Leadership Network statement places a certain equality of blame and concern on Russia and NATO, the fact of the matter is that this group of leading European statesmen are so disturbed that they have come out with this series of reports saying, we are on the cusp of a world war, beginning on European soil, for the third time in the last 100 years.

Just to give you an idea of the level of significance of this statement, the signatories of this taskforce paper, include: Malcolm Rifkind, former foreign and defense secretary of the U.K.; Desmond Brown, former U.K. Defense Secretary; Vyacheslav Trubnikov, former director of Russian Foreign Intelligence; Igor Ivanov, former Russian foreign minister; Adam Daniel Rotfeld, former Polish foreign minister; Paul Quiles, former defense minister of France; former German defense minister Volker Rühe; Ana Palacio, former foreign minister of Spain; Igor Yurgens, chairman of, basically, the board of the Russian Council of Industry and Entrepreneurs; and Hikmet Cetin, former Turkish foreign minister.

In other words, it's a very extensive and actually growing list of European leading diplomats who are frankly scared to death that we're on the cusp of a thermonuclear war, that must be avoided at all costs.

The Levers at Hand

Now, we have obviously, as we've discussed on previous shows, the option of removing President Obama from office immediately under the terms of the 25th Amendment, which was passed by 39 states in 1967 and became part of our Constitution, and lays out detailed procedures where the Cabinet of the President can determine that the President is either physically or mentally incapable of continuing to serve, and can be removed from office. The madness that President Obama is showing in his refusal to back off of the confrontation with Russia, qualifies as the kind of insanity that in the past, in the case of Richard Nixon, was part of the equation that led to forcing his resignation.

Now, there's also another situation that we've also discussed in the recent period, but which now takes on special significance. And that is the fact that former Secretary of State Hillary Clinton knows where the bodies are buried in the Obama Administration. She knows what occurred on the night of Sept. 11, 2012, when President Obama ordered her to cover up the fact that a terrorist attack, coming from terrorist networks that had been built up with U.S. de facto assistance, had assassinated the U.S. Ambassador to Libya, Chris Stevens, and three other American officials.

Now, this issue with Hillary Clinton takes on a special immediacy for two reasons. Number one, the Benghazi Select Committee has accelerated its timetable for investigation, and two of former Secretary of State Clinton's top aides when she was at the State Department—her Chief of Staff Cheryl Mills, and her chief national security advisor Jake Sullivan—will be testifying under oath next Thursday and Friday (Sept. 3 and 4) before Trey Gowdy's Benghazi Select Committee. So there's no question that the events of Sept. 11, 2012 will be a major focus, and the question of the phone call by President Obama to Secretary of State Clinton will almost certainly come up in that questioning.

Now it also happens to be the case that this past week, President Obama personally, and the entire White House team, effectively declared war against Hillary Clinton's candidacy for President. They've been behind the promotion of Joe Biden as an alternative to Hillary Clinton. President Obama, Valerie Jarrett, other Obama intimates, have been involved non-stop in arranging for major financial contributors, including some that have already been pledged to Hillary Clinton, to shift over to backing Joe Biden. Last weekend there was a meeting between Sen. Elizabeth Warren and Joe Biden, prompting speculation about a Biden-Warren ticket, and the fact of that meeting taking place was immediately leaked out, within hours of the meeting happening. So,

is there any reason any longer for Hillary Clinton to have any illusions that there's anything other than an all-out Obama assault against the Clinton family, against her candidacy? And the rest is obvious.

Now, in the middle of this past week, Lyndon LaRouche issued a powerful statement which is now circulating internationally, and is particularly circulating in New York City, in Manhattan, because within a matter of days, world leaders will be descending on New York, beginning in the middle of September, for the United Nations General Assembly. Russian President Putin has announced that he will be personally in New York, and there are some indications that Putin has sent word through the Lavrov-Kerry channels, that he would be open to a face-to-face meeting with President Obama, clearly reflecting the fact that the Russians are profoundly aware of the war provocations coming out of the White House.

But in that context Mr. LaRouche said that the only framework for solving these problems is to accept the fact that Wall Street and London, and the entire trans-Atlantic financial system, are hopelessly, irreversibly bankrupt, and the only solution is to act pre-emptively with an immediate Glass-Steagall reinstatement here in the United States, but immediately followed by Glass-Steagall on a global scale.

Unsurvivable

A dark, gruesome, but wholly true depiction of the threat of thermonuclear war, its consequences, and Obama's deployment of a major portion of the U.S. thermonuclear capabilities in multiple theaters threatening both Russia and China.

http://larouchepac.com/unsurvivable

Every Day Counts
In Today's Showdown
To Save Civilization

That's why you need *EIR's* **Daily Alert Service**, a strategic overview compiled with the input of Lyndon LaRouche, and delivered to your email 5 days a week.

For example: On July 27 Lyndon LaRouche identified this August as a period of maximum danger that President Barack Obama will launch provocations against Russia that could lead to the thermonuclear extinction of mankind.

EIR's July 28 Alert featured LaRouche's evaluation, along with critical intelligence on the Russian strategic doctrine. Throughout the rest of the week, the Alert has pointed to the way Hillary Clinton's exposure of Obama could interrupt Obama's war drive—as well as updates on the worsening threat.

This is intelligence you need to act on, if we are going to survive as a nation and a species. Can you really afford to be without it?

EIR Rededicates Itself To a Principle

by Tony Papert

Sept. 1—*EIR* must now rededicate ourselves to a principle which our great Founder, Lyndon H. LaRouche, Jr., has been working to elicit from within us for now half a century. That principle is that the only effective form of human action, is that which is characterized by discovery of a new principle, like a new physical principle of the universe. Indeed, such discovery is in fact the only human form of action.

Not merely over the past many years, but, more embarrassingly even over the past weeks, *EIR* has been guilty of emulating the ideas-free "journalism" of our "Brand X" competition. Never again!

Arguing again along these lines one week ago, LaRouche said, "You'll find much of the history of mankind corresponds to that. Now, what's the method: The method is the development *of method*, of scientific method. It's not the application of scientific method, it's the *concept* of scientific method. And all the ideas of these practical systems,—practical, practical, practical,—is crap! And we shouldn't encourage it. What's science? How did Kepler produce science? Did he go and build in some large projects, as such, construction projects? No. Not at all. What happened is, the scientist *per se*, the *scientist per se*, not the practical engineering person, the scientist *per se*.

"Physical science, the human practice of physical science, is not based on the fruit of physical science as such; it's based on the *addition of new levels* of physical science. It lies with Einstein. And most people today don't know what Einstein meant, and therefore they say they're practical, that they can do practical things.

"The Astronomer" by Dutch painter Johannes Vermeer, finished in 1668.

That's because they can only say that because they're incompetent."

To signal, to guide, and to embody this rededication of ours, we are publishing below a pioneering, deeply-researched account of the role of General of the Armies Douglas MacArthur,—beyond compare the greatest military genius of the Twentieth Century,—in World War I.

MacArthur and America's Two-Front War

by Dean Andromidas and Don Phau

Aug. 20—On August 16, 1962, President John F. Kennedy held his second meeting with General of the Armies Douglas MacArthur. In the course of a wide-ranging discussion Kennedy asked MacArthur the following question:

> I was wondering, having read that [The Guns of August], whether in reading some other things—whether you thought the leadership by the British and the French was wholly incompetent, and left, particularly in '17 (1917) with Passchendaele and all these tremendous casualties for 8,9,10 miles—from what—June till October, November? Was there any alternative action by the Allies? Do you think they had to continue those assaults on those trenches, or was there anything else they could have done?

White House

President John Kennedy has lunch with General Douglas MacArthur, July 20, 1961.

MacArthur answers:

> I would have handled the campaign in a completely different way. With modern weapons, with the machine guns, and even the weapons which we had not talked about since 1917, frontal assaults were nothing but suicide. You must envelop. You must hit the lines of supply. There's no other way to victory. You'll have one of these tremendous assaults that go ahead and gain 3 or 4 kilometers. They'd be so decimated, and so exhausted and everything, that they couldn't be exploited.
>
> And both sides made the same mistake. The Germans made exactly the same mistake. He [was] down there when he made that great attack through Champagne, we just slaughtered him. My division was right in the middle on the day they fought the French army at that time. I put all … I put every gun of my artillery brigade on the line of the infantry, all the colonels of the brigade commanding just sweated blood. But we put them in there. And they just mowed those people down. You couldn't get—nothing could penetrate.
>
> Now the firepower is so much greater that a frontal assault is just suicide. I'm sure that the British … They were under the influence, the old Wellington influence. And those soldiers that Wellington had, they were all volunteers,

you understand. You only had about 60,000, small forces compared to that. And they were always magnificent. They could make a frontal assault that was always exceptional. Always they won on the peninsula. Always they licked the French. Always they licked everybody. And they had an idea that bravery, courage, and to face with your breast and go on with the drums beating and the fifes blowing and everything that they'd roll along. There never was any great leadership on the Western Front by the British during the war. Douglas Haig I knew well. He was a good, cautious, average type of, well, a pragmatic soldier. But the ... There was nothing ... There was no spark that was shown anyplace.

Now in the French, they had some leaders who were magnificent. [Marshal Ferdinand] Foch himself I rate as a great captain. [Marshal Philippe Henri] Pétain was timid. He was something like [British Field Marshal Bernard Law] Montgomery. He always could see how he couldn't do it, but never could quite see how he could do it. But they had men like [General Henri] Gouraud, who was magnificent, of the leaders I have known anyplace, anywhere. [General Jean] Degoutte. Oh, they had a number of them. The French leadership was not lacking, but the French leadership in the Second World War was beneath contempt.[1]

When the United States entered World War I, it was not as an "ally" of the so-called "Allied" powers, but as an "Associated Power" because, other than defeating Germany, it did not, officially, share in the war aims of those powers. The "Allies" saw the war as a principal means of destroying their main rival Germany, which would enable a redivision of the global assets as outlined in the secret treaties like the 1916 Sykes Picot, which divided up the Middle East between Britain and France. For MacArthur's faction, their forecast was far more foreboding, as they saw the defeat of Germany opening the way to the British Empire to organize a new entente against the United States, which had to

1. This interchange is reported in: John F. Kennedy Presidential Recordings, Kennedy Conversation on Aug. 16, 1962 (12); Conversation with General Douglas MacArthur: http://web1.millercenter.org/presidentialrecordings/jfk_1_pub/18_aug16.pdf

fight the war with this forecast constantly in mind. The war had to be conducted such that the early defeat of Germany would put the United States in a position to dictate a peace that would secure the interests of the United States, whose interests were diametrically opposite to those of the British Empire and their would-be allies. As we shall see, the U.S. military did its part towards this goal, in which MacArthur's role was important, only to see it squandered, undermined and destroyed by Wilson and "colonel" Edward House. This would serve as a bitter lesson to be corrected two decades later by FDR and MacArthur.

America's Principles of War

The principles laid down by the military, which were shared by Secretary of War Newton Baker, were roughly as follows:

First: the war will be won in Europe on the Western Front. The United States will not send its troops for major operations on other fronts, would further press to assure that the "Allied Powers" would not expand any efforts beyond the Western Front.

This became a major point of contention after the Russian Revolution and Russia's leaving the war. Churchill and the British government led a campaign to withdraw troops from the Western Front to establish a new front in the East, which in reality was to crush Soviet Russia. Lloyd George wanted to allow Japan to deploy 2.5 million troops to occupy all of the Russian Empire east of the Ural Mountains. U.S. General Tasker Bliss was to comment that if that were to happen, the Japanese would never leave. This became a major issue for the U.S. military, since such a Japanese move was seen to be laying the ground for a major threat to the United States once Germany was defeated, by consolidating an Anglo-Japanese entente against the United States. The United States therefore prevented this new front from forming. The United States participation in the anti-Soviet so-called "intervention" that did take place, was small and highly restricted, and in reality had as its purpose the prevention of British plans to divide Russia between the British Empire and the Japanese Empire.

Second: the United States would deploy an independent army with its own territorial front and not become auxiliaries of the British and French by sending regiments to be integrated into and serve under Anglo-French command. This was not simply to maintain self-respect: more important, with its own independent army, the United States could most effectively assure that all effort would be exerted on the Western Front, and allow it to earn the necessary prestige in the eyes of the European population so that it could play a decisive role in organizing the postwar peace. The military's plans foresaw the United States deploying five million men to Europe by the Summer of 1919, a force larger than the combined armies of Britain and France, which would put the United States in the strongest position in negotiating a peace that would protect American interests.

Thirdly, and this is the importance of an independent army—the United States would do everything possible to put an end to the meat grinder of "trench warfare," and revert once again to an "open warfare" of rapid movements and flanking action.

Fourth was the naming of an Allied Commander, under whom the United States, France, and Great Britain would coordinate a common strategy. It should be noted that this did not exist prior to the U.S. entry into the war, so that both Britain and France were launching independent offensives without even coordinating with one another.

MacArthur was intimately aware of, and supportive of these goals; in fact he had helped to formulate them. It will be seen that the United States was in reality fighting a two-front war. One against Germany, which was the easy one, the second with the Allies who were pursuing a new "Thirty Years War." The Allies wanted American money and American blood, whereby American soldiers would be directly integrated into allied divisions under British and French command, and thus fall victim to the organized butchery they called warfare.

MacArthur's Role in Preparing for War

Once War was declared in April of 1917, MacArthur had already participated in many of the decisions taken to prepare the army for war, from his position as a junior

Library of Congress

Newton D. Baker, Secretary of War from March 1916 to March 1921.

officer on the General Staff.

In March 1916, Newton D. Baker, a Democrat and former mayor of Cleveland, had become Secretary of War. MacArthur, who was assigned by the General Staff to serve as Baker's military assistant, had this to say about him in his memoirs: "diminutive in size, but large in heart, with a clear, brilliant mind, and a fine ability to make instant and positive decisions, he was to become one of the U.S.'s greatest War Secretaries."[2]

On June 30, 1916, MacArthur had become Baker's military assistant and chief of the Bureau of Information of the War Department, in effect, the liaison with the press and press censor. In this period the question of "preparedness" and preliminary reorganization and expansion of the Army as well as the Navy began. In fact, a major naval construction program was begun. In this context there was a debate on whether to deploy the National Guard if the United States entered the war. While some of the General Staff were opposed, MacArthur and Baker called for its deployment, which was accepted.

Baker was always up against the Anglophiles inside and outside the Wilson Administration. One of these was U.S. Ambassador to London, Walter Hines Page, who many considered represented the British cause in Washington rather than the American cause in London. While Baker disliked "Colonel" Edward House's influence on Wilson, Hines Page was so anglophile that he even upset Wilson. One biographer of Baker said that Baker agreed with U.S. Secretary of the Navy Josephus Daniels, who said this about Page: Wilson was "so incensed at Page's partisanship with Great Britain that any recommendation of Page's irritated rather than convinced him. This irritation was all the greater because of his long friendship for Page and real affection for him. He felt, and had good grounds for thinking so,

2. MacArthur, Douglas, *Reminiscences* (U.S.Naval Institute Press, January 1, 1964, republished April 15, 2012), page 50.

that Page… did not represent the United States in England but represented the British Government and took his cue from it."[3]

Another Anglophile whom Baker learned to dislike was Teddy Roosevelt, who, despite his advanced age and great weight, demanded that he resurrect the "Rough Riders" and be given a commission to fight in the war. TR cited the fact that as President he had been at one time "commander in chief" of the armed forces. Baker, Wilson, and Pershing refused such approaches, not only because of the absurdity of TR as a military commander, but out of fear was that if he had any official standing, TR would deploy to Paris at a time when "Washington was trying to protect purely American interests against enthusiastic concessions… to keep things humming." In fact, according to one biographer Baker thought TR was "insane enough to die in restraint, possibly a straight jacket."[4]

Needless to say, both Lloyd George and Clemenceau hated Baker as they did General Pershing and the whole American Expeditionary Force (AEF) he headed.

When the United States declared war on April 6, 1917, the General Staff proposed sending only an army of 500,000 men. MacArthur and Baker opposed this, calling for an unlimited number as well as the deployment of the National Guard. The reasons are obvious. With an army of 500,000 men, the U.S, army would become an auxiliary of the allies and have zero influence on the execution of the war.

Baker opposed a "volunteer" army and supported the draft. He cited the British volunteer system, which whipped the population into a "frenzy" with "orators preaching hate of the Germans, and newspapers exaggerating enemy outrages to make men enlist out of motives of revenge and retaliation."[5]

Following discussions between Baker and MacArthur, Major General John Pershing, a protégé of Douglas MacArthur's father, General Arthur MacArthur, and the youngest and most competent of the Major Generals in the army at the time, was chosen to head the AEF. MacArthur had great respect for Pershing from the time he had first met him in his father's office, when his father was stationed in California. MacArthur wrote that he consulted with him throughout his career, even when he himself was Chief of Staff. MacArthur mentions that when he was wrestling with the question of transforming the cavalry to armored and mechanized warfare, and came up against resistance within the Army, he consulted with and received the backing of Pershing. In his memoirs, MacArthur has this to say about Pershing:

> General Pershing's fame rests largely on his personal character. He was not a genius at strategy and his tactical experience was limited, but in his indomitable will for victory, in his implacable belief in the American soldier; in his invincible resistance to all attempts to exploit or patronize the American army, he rose to the highest flights of his profession. He inspired self-respect for our national forces and a foreign recognition of our military might which was properly placed as fully equal to the best of the human race. My memories of him sustained and strengthened me during many a lonely and bitter moment of the Pacific and Korean Wars….[6]

It is this fight, led by Pershing, for the recognition of the military might and capabilities of the American Army, which is the context for MacArthur's heroism as a subordinate officer in his capacity as Chief of Staff of a Division, and later Brigade Commander. In the two-front war Pershing was leading, any victory and demonstration of the competence and superior fighting capacity of American military power was crucial in the fight on the second front, against British and French policy. It is safe to assume that MacArthur fully grasped this most important of all issues in conducting the war.

Conflicts with the British

Baker fully supported his generals, especially Pershing and Chief of Staff General Payton March, both of whom were protégés of Arthur MacArthur and close to the younger MacArthur, in their determination for the United States to have a fully separate Army and territorial front. The arguments between the Americans and the British and French were famous throughout the war. Pershing's steadfastness at the meetings of the allied military command councils and earned him the hatred of British Prime Minister David Lloyd George and

---

3. Cramer, C.H., *Newton D. Baker: A Biography* (The World Publishing Company), page 90.
4. Cramer, *ibid.*, 113.
5. *Ibid.*, 96.

---

6. *Ibid.*, 56.

Major General John Pershing (right), head of the American Expeditionary Force, with French Marshal Ferdinand Foch, Commander-in-Chief of the Allied Armies in World War I, sometime in 1918.

Marshall Douglas Haig. Baker joined in that fight whenever necessary, and once told Lloyd George, who had "advised" Baker to put U.S. soldiers under British command: "If we want advice about who should command our armies, we would ask for it. But until then we do not want nor need it from anyone, least of all you."

"Colonel" Edward House, being a British agent, fully supported the British on this question and tried to convince Baker. On July 18, 1917 Baker wrote House to rebuff this suggestion and explain why an American army had to have its own doctrine, secure a place at the front, and operate independently. "This puts us into the war as a great power conducting *pro tanto* a war of our own," he said. The United States would retain its identity and remain uncommitted to Britain or France after the war. Thus, America could work out its own peace plans. "Complete diplomatic and military individuality, if not independence, will then [after the war] be of great importance to us."

The determination for the creation of an independent American Army was at the center of the U.S. prepara-

tion for war. The General Staff drafted the "30 Division Plan." Since American divisions comprised a complement of over 20,000 men, they were twice the strength of French, British, and German divisions. Comprised of two brigades, these divisions were almost the size of a French and British corps. Thus thirty American divisions were the equivalent of 60 European, and would be the size of the British expeditionary force in France.

Furthermore the plan called for the arrival of 1,328,448 men in France by December 31, 1918. Not only had this been surpassed by August, but in July 1918 an "80 Division plan" was approved and began to be implemented. If the war had gone into 1919, the American army would have out-numbered the combined forces of France and Great Britain!

It was suspected that maybe Lloyd George and Clemenceau were getting second thoughts about American involvement in the war. This was reflected in the foot-dragging by the British in supplying shipping for the transportation of the American Army and its equipment. The U.S. Merchant Marine was not sufficient. Although a Liberty Ship-type mass production of cargo and troop-carrying ships was immediately launched when the war broke out, only a few ships were finished prior to the end of the war.

Pershing had this to say about the failure of British and French to supply shipping:

> The question, in its finality, was, therefore, one of sea transportation; but so far all efforts to get the allies, especially the British, to consider giving help to bring over men and supplies had been futile. They did not seem to realize that America would be practically negligible from a military standpoint unless the Allies could provide shipping. Nor did they seem to appreciate that time was a vital factor. But the spirit of full cooperation among the Allies did not then exist. They seemed to regard the transportation of an American army overseas as entirely our affair. This apparent indifference also gave further color to the suspicion that perhaps an American army as such was not wanted.[7]

Another thorny issue involved the deployment of the National Guard. It was decided that the third Amer-

---

7. Pershing, John, *My Experiences in the World War* (New York: Frederick A. Stokes Co. Vol. I), page 95.

American troops parade through Paris upon their arrival July 4, 1918, to what General Pershing characterized as "joyful acclaim."

ican division to be deployed would be comprised of National Guard members. But, if such a division was drawn from just one state, it could have negative political consequences. On the one hand, the other states might consider it as a biased move in favor of a single state. On the other hand, if that division suffered huge losses or other catastrophes, this would have a political blowback effect on the war effort. Therefore Baker and MacArthur conceived of the 42 "Rainbow" national guard division as one that would draw units from states throughout the union, stretching, as MacArthur himself said in his discussions with Baker, like a rainbow across the United States. Baker chose MacArthur to become the division's chief of staff, promoting him two grades, from Major to full Colonel. Brig. General William Mann, the head of the militia department of the War Department, was named commander. But he was one year away from retirement and not physically fit. In fact, he was not really fit to command, so MacArthur basically ran the division until it was deployed to France, soon after which Mann was replaced by Major General Charles T. Menoher. The Rainbow would become one of the four or five really crack divisions of the AEF.

This issue of fitness to command among the senior officers who were a few years away from retirement, as with all wars, was a crucial one, because younger officers possessing both vigor and an aggressive intelli-

gence were required if war was to be carried out successfully.

Pershing himself called for weeding out old and incompetent or physically unfit officers from troop commands in France, because of the harsh and rigorous conditions of modern war. He pointed out that the French and British had very few division commanders over 45 years of age, and very few brigadiers over 40.

MacArthur Arrives in France

The question of the need for the AEF to earn the United States the "prestige" that was necessary to impact the postwar settlement, is reflected in this description by Pershing of the first appearance of American troops in Paris on July 4, 1918, following three years of slaughter because of the incompetence of the British and French leaders.

> The first appearance of American combat troops brought forth joyful acclaim from the people. On the march to Lafayette's tomb at Picpus Cemetery the battalion was jointed by a great crowd.... With wreaths about their necks and bouquets in their hats and rifles, the column looked like a moving flower garden. With only a semblance of military formation, the animated throng pushed through avenues of people to the martial strains of the French band and the still more thrilling

music of cheering voices....
The humbler folk of Paris seemed to look upon these few hundred of our stalwart fighting men as their real deliverance. Many people dropped on their knees in reverence as the column went by. These stirring scenes conveyed vividly the emotions of a people to whom the outcome of the war had seemed all but hopeless.

The 42nd division and its Chief of Staff MacArthur sailed to France on October 18. One of the naval escorts was the *Chattanooga*, commanded by his brother, Captain Arthur MacArthur. Fourteen days later they landed at St Nazaire, France. Following a short and incomplete period of further training, four regiments of the division were placed under the command of General Georges de Bazelaire of the French VII Army Corps, to be battle-trained with four French divisions. General Mann was retired and replaced by General Charles T. Menoher, highly respected by MacArthur and a classmate of Pershing. Menoher preferred to supervise the division from headquarters, where he could keep in constant touch with the corps and the army, relying on MacArthur to handle the battle line.

The 42nd carried out this mission under the following orders by General Pershing: "In military operations against the Imperial German Government you are directed to cooperate with the forces of the other countries employed against the enemy; but in so doing the underlying ideas must be kept in view that the forces of the United States are a separate and distinct component of the combined forces, the identity of which must be preserved. This fundamental rule is subject to such minor exceptions in particular circumstances as your judgement may approve. The decision as to when your command or any of its party is ready for action is confided to you, and you will exercise full discretion in determining the manner of cooperation...."

The other crucial issue was the fight against the self-

The "self-slaughter" of trench warfare during World War I.

clipart.com

slaughter of trench warfare. Up until the time of U.S. entry into the conflict, the war had been nothing less then a series of massive war crimes, not just against respective enemies but against their allies' own men. The use of artillery barrages accounted for 87 percent of the casualties of war, with the average casualty rate reaching 38 percent, one third of which would be deaths. The British at the Battle of the Somme suffered 60,000 casualties on the first day, 20,000 of which were deaths. This is not to mention the gross crimes of the First Sea Lord Winston Churchill and his infamous Dardenelles-Gallipoli campaign (1915-16), which ended in the sinking of six capital ships, the slaughter of tens of thousands of British, French and Allied troops, and an ignoble defeat. These troops could have otherwise been deployed in France if the Allies actually wanted to end the war.

The AEF always had as its major goal a return to the "open warfare" of rapid movements and flanking actions. This was an issue at every echelon of the army, from the level of army group which should seek to outflank the enemy's entire front, to the twelve-man squad which could use flanking maneuvers to take out a machinegun nest. A conflict arise because the United States had to resort to using British and French instructors in the beginning of the war. But these instructors taught tactics for "trench warfare," which were no tactics at all, but in many cases, simply training soldiers to jump out of their trenches and advance forward in some organized formation. Contrast this to what the U.S. army called "minor tactics," where even the twelve-man squad is trained in skirmishing tactics of rapid motions and mini-flanking operations; who are well-trained in the use of their rifles, and capable of organizing the rapid defense of areas they have conquered.

The Rainbow's 165th Infantry regiment, also known as the "fighting 69th," called these minor tactics "Indian style" warfare. George Patton, who was a sort of genius on the battlefield, but who would become more of an opinionated jerk the further he got from a battlefield, nonetheless aptly described these minor tactic when he said, "first, we are going to grab the enemy by the nose and then kick him in the pants." In other words, aggressively attack the enemy while at the same time looking for the opportunity to outflank him

Commenting on this problem in a communication to the War Department that was using French and British instructors in the training of American officers in the United States, Pershing wrote,

My cable stated that too much tutelage by Allied officers tended to rob our officers of a sense of responsibility and initiative. It was well known that many of these [French and British] officers sent to the States were not professional soldiers, but were men whose knowledge was limited to personal experience in subordinate grades in trench warfare. Moreover, the French doctrine, as well as the British, was based upon the cautious advance of infantry with prescribed objectives, where obstacles had been destroyed and resistance largely broken by artillery. The French infantryman, as has been already stated, did not rely upon his rifle and made little use of its great power. The infantry of both the French and the British were poor skirmishers as a result of extended service in the trenches. Our mission required an aggressive offensive based on self-reliant infantry.

The organization of our army was radically different from that of any of the Allied armies and we could not become imitators of methods which applied especially to armies in which initiative was more or less repressed by infinite attention to detail in directives prepared for their guidance. It was our belief... that efficiency could be attained only by adherence to our own doctrines based upon thorough appreciation of the American temperament, qualifications and deficiencies. I recommended the withdrawal of all instruction in the United States from the hands of Allied instructors. This recommendation was promptly approved by the Chief of Staff, who entirely agreed with my view.

Needless to say, Pershing conceived what he believed to be a war-winning strategy for an independent U.S. Army on the Western Front. Up until then, the front had stretched from the Swiss border, northwestward along a line through France, Luxembourg, and Belgium to the channel. Various Allied and German offensives had been launched along this line. But the most strategically vulnerable part of this front for the Germans lay in front of Metz, which was the sector of the front closest to Germany, and was in fact the main avenue of entry into the very heart of Germany. If one passes Metz, one direction leads you directly to the Rhine valley in the region of Frankfurt, and on to Berlin. The other direction, down the Moselle River, leads you to the Ruhrgebiet, Germany's industrial heartland. Furthermore, Metz and the city of Sedan, further west along the front, served as the crucial railheads for the sophisticated network of railroads and hard surface roads that Germany used to supply their entire front extending to the English Channel. Capture this sector and the entire German line crumbles much like the famous Inchon strategy.

In the opposite direction, is the road directly to Paris. Germany well understood this, and this was the chief reasoning behind its ill-fated Verdun offensive.

In laying out his conception, Pershing wrote:

...Therefore on the active front anywhere west of the Argonne Forest there would have been little space or opportunity for the strategical employment of our arms.

On the battlefront from Argonne Forest to Vosages Mountains a chance for the decisive use of our army was very clearly presented. The enemy's positions cover not only the coal fields of the Saar but also the important Longwy-Briey iron-ore region. Moreover, behind this front lay the vital portion of his rail communications connecting the garrison at Metz with the Armies in

FIGURE 1

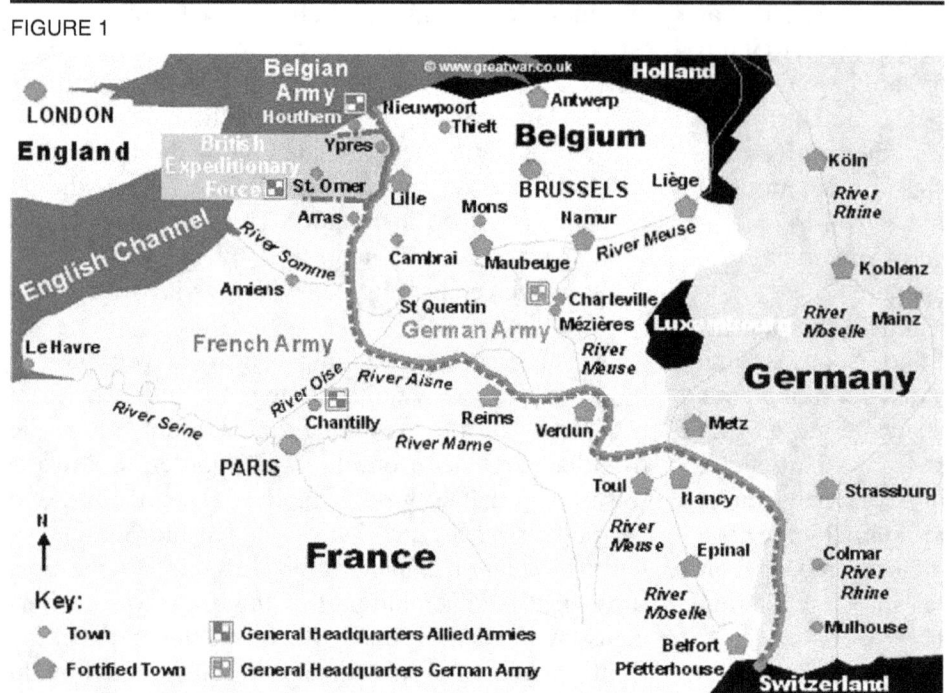

An overview of the battlefield on the Western Front, showing the battlefront between the German and Allied forces.

the west. A deep allied advance on this front and the seizure of the Longwy-Briey section would deprive the enemy an indisputable supply of ore for the manufacture of munitions. It might also lead to the invasion of enemy territory in the Moselle valley and endanger the supply of coal in the Saar basin. Allied success here would also cut his line of communications between the east and the west and compel his withdrawal from northern France or force his surrender.

Under the circumstance, the enemy could but regard the Verdun salient as threatening this sensitive area in the event that the Allies should find themselves capable of taking the offensive on that front. It was his desire to improve his position and also his prestige that prompted his violent and persistent attack in the attempt in 1916 to capture Verdun.[8]

As we will see, these words would almost become prophetic.

For reasons unknown, by 1917 this region, the most vulnerable for both France and Germany, was considered a "quiet zone" where both sides seemed to main-

tain a tense status quo rather than pursue serious operations. On February 13, 1918, after a period of a few months training, Pershing ordered the 42nd to move to the front at the Luneville sector of Southern Lorraine for a month's training with the French VII Corps.

Prior to entering the line in a quiet sector, an inspection of the 42nd by the AEF staff revealed some serious deficiencies among its regimental commanders, some of whom had to be replaced for incompetence. Many of these officers were not from the regular army, and had other deficiencies as well. This was the key reason MacArthur felt he had to be in a hands-on position during operations, to provide encouragement, and if necessary, direction. He was not some bullet-head wanting to be where the action was, and to get loaded up with medals for bravery, but saw it as a necessary part of his mission to overcome the inherent deficiencies in his very young and inexperienced division. Furthermore, success on the German front was crucial for success on the other front: winning the respect of the Allied officers and men as part of the fight for an independent U.S. Army that could act decisively and determine the course of the war.

As divisional Chief of Staff, MacArthur was considered as highly competent, and according to his military aide Captain Wolf, "MacArthur worked very early in the morning on his field plans. Alone, he made notes on a card, and by the time we met for a staff discussion he had the plans all worked out.... His plans invariably covered the optimum situation as well as the minimum. He was meticulous in organization and consummate in planning."[9] This enabled him to deploy himself on the front.

MacArthur's first action at the front came quickly when he decided to join a French raid:

_____

8. *Ibid.*, 83-84.

_____

9. James, D. Clayton, *The Years of MacArthur, Vol. I 1880-1941* (Boston: Houghton Mifflin Co., 1970), 156.

On February 26th I had my first contact with German troops. I had long felt it was imperative to know by personal observation what the division had to face. It is all very well to make a perfect plan of attack, to work out in theory foolproof design for victory. But if that plan does not consider the calibre of troops, the terrain to be fought over, the enemy strength opposed, then it may become confused and fail. I went to see General De Bazelaire, but he was reluctant to authorize me to join a French raiding party out to capture Boche prisoners, I told him frankly, "I cannot fight them if I cannot see them." He understood, and told me to go.[10]

Brigadier General Douglas MacArthur receives one of his two Distinguished Service Crosses, won for his valor in World War I.

MacArthur went on that raid with veteran French soldiers, in what became a very savage fight which nonetheless ended in a success. He received the Croix de Guerre from de Bazelaire and a Silver Star from the American commander, which MacArthur himself said was "a bit too much" for him. Nonetheless it was the first, though small, victory in the U.S. Army's two-front war.

The division's first attack took place in March. It was to be a raid on the German trenches by the division's 168th Infantry regiment, and as MacArthur, who accompanied it, wrote, "millions of people, friend and foe, waited breathlessly for the first news of an American attack."

Following the initiating of the attack, a German artillery barrage was laid on them. "Our casualties began to mount. I began to feel uneasy. You never really know about men at such a time. They were not professionals. Few of them had ever been under fire. I decided to walk the line, hoping that my presence might comfort the men."

The men did not fail, and the success won both MacArthur and the regiment's commander, Major Charles J. Casey, the Distinguished Service Cross, the second highest military award below the Medal of Honor.

In his evaluation of MacArthur, Divisional Commander General Menoher wrote, "On this occasion, in the face of the determined and violent resistance of an alert enemy, he lent actual advice on the spot to unit commanders and by his supervision of the operations not only guaranteed its success, but left with the entire division the knowledge of the constant attention of their leaders to their problems in action, and the sense of security which his wise and courageous leadership there impressed on the engaged companies."[11]

On March 19, 1918, MacArthur gave Secretary of War Baker a tour of this front. Back in Washington, Baker would tell journalists that MacArthur was the "greatest fighting frontline general" in Pershing's army.[12]

The importance of MacArthur's hands-on approach was underscored by the evaluation of the Division by Lt. Col. Hugh A. Drum, who, while giving MacArthur high praise, pointed out there was "failure on the part of officers to look for and sometimes to correct errors of tactics and discipline. The principle of teaching constant observation for errors and correction of faults has not been developed sufficiently in this division." Nonetheless he noted that the division has "made a very favorable impression on the French and performed its work with excellent spirit and aggressiveness...."[13]

Taking over No-Man's Land

On March 31, 1918, the Germans launched an offensive they hoped would win the war. They targeted

---

10. MacArthur, op. cit.

11. James, *op. cit.*, 159.
12. *Ibid.*, 160.
13. *Ibid.*, 161.

the British 5th Army, 170 miles to the left of the 42nd. Then there was a strike towards the French lines on the Marne and Paris. The four French divisions that had been stationed with the 42nd were withdrawn to be deployed in a counter-attack, leaving the Lorraine front in the hand of the 42nd for the next 82 days.

The 42nd relieved three French divisions who had held the Baccarat sector. The so called "quiet" sector became a lot noisier once the 42nd arrived, because they used the opportunity for live combat training by "taking over" no-man's land. Over three months the division conducted over 90 raids.

When the division was relieved, French General Pierre

French General Henri Gouraud, considered by MacArthur to be "the greatest" of modern French commanders.

Georges Duport, under whose corps command the 42nd served, cited the division for its "offensive ardour, the sense for the utilization and the organization of terrain as for the liaison of the arms, the spirit of method, the discipline shown by all its officers and men, the inspiration animating them, [which] prove that at the first call, they can henceforth take a glorious place in the new line of battle."[14]

Father Duffy, senior Irish Catholic Chaplin of the Division and great friend of the 165th regiment, the so-called fighting Irish, in which the very aggressive and intelligent Major William Donovan commanded a battalion, had this to say about MacArthur at Baccarat:

> Our Chief of staff chafes at his own task of directing instead of fighting, and he has pushed himself into raids and forays in which, some older heads think, he had no business to be. His admirers say that his personal boldness has a very valuable result in helping to give confidence to the men. Colonel [Frank R.] McCoy and Major [William J.] Donovan are strong on this point. Donovan says it would be a blamed

good thing for the army if some General got himself shot in the front line. General Menoher and General Lenihan approve in secret of these madnesses; but all five of them are wild Celts, whose opinion no sane man like myself would uphold.[15]

These four months gave the 42nd the live training that turned it into one of the AEF's crack divisions. Colonel Henry J. Reilly, commander of the 149 Field Artillery, commented that this period demonstrated the Division's effectiveness not only to the AEF high command, but to that of the British and French as well: "Of greatest importance, the Rainbow in the course of its tour of duty in Lorraine demonstrated to the French, the British, and to the American high command that American citizen soldiers could take their place beside the best troops the war produced and equal their best performance."

Champagne Marne German Offensive

By June 1918 there were 510,000 U.S. combat troops in France, including 18 full divisions, but only the original four were combat-ready. When the Germans struck at the Aisne-Marne region and advanced to and captured Chateau Thierry only 50 miles from Paris, Pershing committed the 2nd, 26th and the 42nd to aid the French in stopping the German offensive. In July, in preparation to counter a German offensive, the 42nd was assigned to the French Fourth Army under the command of General Henri Gouraud. That same month MacArthur was promoted to Brig. General.

For MacArthur, Gouraud "was the greatest" of the modern French commanders. By contrast Pétain "always exaggerated the enemy potential and thereby failed to exploit fully his successes, and Foch was too inflexible once he had outlined a plan, and consequently

---

14. *Ibid.*, 63.

15. *Ibid.*, 165.

missed opportunities. But Gouraud was without a weakness. I spent much time with him in his headquarters at the Ferme de Suippes and the more I saw him the more I liked him. It became a mutual friendship that lasted until his death many years later."[16]

For his part, Gouraud told Colonel S.L.H. Slocum after the war, "I considered General MacArthur to be one of the finest and bravest officers I have ever served with."[17]

There is a reference in MacArthur's discussion with Kennedy, to how he lined up his division to wait for the German attack. He was actually referring to the tactic that Gouraud had developed to counter the German tactic for forcing a breakthrough on a limited front, in which the Germans bypassed strong points and attack the weakly held rear:

When I reported, he had already worked out a complete new theory of defense against the German tactic of breaking through and then bypassing strong points to exploit the lightly held rear areas. He would vacate his first line of trenches except for skeleton 'suicide squads' who would warn with rocket flares when the enemy's grey clad infantry began their assault. Gouraud would wait until the attack reached his now evacuated first line, then lay down a withering fire, thus destroying the enemy's momentum and solidarity. By the time our main line would be reached, the enemy would be spent and ready for destruction. It was an entirely new concept of trench warfare—a defense in depth which became a death trap for the attack.

But when they met the dikes of our real line, they were exhausted, uncoordinated and scattered, incapable of going further without being reorganized and reinforced... "Their legs are broken," I told our sweating cannoneers.[18]

The German offensive was successfully defeated, and in praise of the 42nd Gouraud said: "We have in our midst in the most perfect fraternity of arms, the 42nd American Division. We esteem it an honor to rival them in courage and nerve. Its men went under fire as at a football game, in shirtsleeves, with the sleeves rolled up over nervous biceps."[19]

The 42nd was then assigned to the French Sixth Army under the command of General Jean Degoutte. On July 23, the 42nd was deployed near Chateau Thierry to relieve the 26th Division. The Germans were already pulling back and they were ordered to pursue. This battle earned MacArthur a fourth silver star, while France made him a member of the Legion of Honor with a second Croix de Guerre.

MacArthur was made commander of the 84th Infantry Brigade of the 42nd Division.

The Fight for the First American Army

Despite his success in stopping the German offensive, General Gouraud's tactics were still very much within the geometry of "trench warfare." His plan did not include the immediate launching of a swift counterattack that could be carried through the German lines. Instead, the lines were again "stabilized" and a separate detailed offensive plan would be drafted again for some limited fixed objective to be implemented at some future point, giving the Germans time to re-establish their lines of defense.

Up until this point American divisions and brigades fought within French and British corps or divisions. Invariably, wherever they fought, they not only gave a good showing for themselves, but had a remoralizing effect on Allied soldiers, especially the French. With over one million men now in France, Pershing made the decision to fight for the formation of an independent American army with an independent territorial front. That front, Pershing reasoned, would have to be in front of Metz at the St. Mihiel salient, precisely the point which Pershing had earlier reasoned could become the decisive sector to break the German front and roll up the entire German line.

Pershing opened this fight for an independent Army at the Allied Conference of Commanders in Chief at Foch's headquarters on July 24, 1918. On the same day, Pershing issued orders for the formation of the First American Army to take effect Aug. 10, 1918, "Not only was it demanded by the existing situation," Pershing wrote, "but by all the circumstances of our participation in the war. Not the least important consideration was that until such an army should be actually formed and successfully carried out an operation, our

16. MacArthur, *op. cit.*,64.
17. James, *op. cit.*, 176.
18. MacArthur, *op. cit.*, 64-65.

19. *Ibid.*, 65.

position before our people at home would not be enviable."[20]

At the same time the British kept insisting that the U.S. troops be sent to support the White Russian armies. Despite his opposition, Pershing was forced by the White House to send a token force of one regiment to Murmansk. Nonetheless, Pershing was backed by this statement from the Administration, probably issued under pressure from Baker, entitled "Aims and purposes of the U.S.," which was sent to the Ambassadors of Great Britain, France, and Italy, reiterating the U.S. commitment to win the war and calling them to "accept its deliberate judgment that it should not dissipate its forces by attempting important operations elsewhere...." As for Russia "it was clear that intervention was out of the question as it would serve no useful purpose nor be of advantage in the prosecution of the War."

In a letter to Secretary Baker on July 28, 1918, Pershing laid out this new fight:

On July 23rd, when Mr. Clemenceau was at my headquarters for the conference, I had an opportunity to speak about the use of our troops. I told him they were being wasted and that instead of the Allies being always on the defensive, an American Army should be formed at once to strike an offensive blow and turn the tide of the war. He was very much impressed at such boldness, as he had heard only of our men going into French divisions as platoons [an obvious lie] or at most as regiments. Soon after that, Pétain was called to Paris and I have heard he was told my views. Anyway, Pétain soon began to take another view.

Our troops have done well for new troops and the part they have taken has encouraged our allies, especially the French, to go in and help put over a counteroffensive. This offensive, between Soissons and Chateau-Thierry, was planned some time ago, to be undertaken south of the Marne; or to the east between the Marne and Reims. I had conferred with General Pétain and had arranged to put the 1st, 2nd, and 26th Divisions in the attack north of the Marne. As it turned out, all of these troops were engaged with results you already know. The participation by our troops made this offensive possible and in fact the brunt of it

fell to them. Our divisions in this advance outstepped the French and had to slow down their speed occasionally for them to catch up.

Two American corps are now organized and on the active front. There are to be organized into the Field Army, which will take its place in line under my immediate command on August 10th. We shall occupy a sector north of the Marne and probably replace the 6th French Army. So that before long I shall have to relinquish command of the Field Amy and command the Group [of Armies].

I have had to insist very strongly, in face of determined opposition, to get our troops out of leading strings. You know the French and British have always advanced the idea that we should not form divisions until our men had three or four months with them. We have found, however, that only a short time was necessary to learn all they know, as it is confined to trench warfare almost entirely, and I have insisted on open warfare training. To get this training, it has been necessary to unite our men under our own commanders, which is now being done rapidly.

The additional fact that training with these worn-out French and British troops, if continued, is detrimental, is another reason for haste in forming our own units and conducting our own training. The morale of the Allies is low and association with them has had a bad effect upon our men. To counteract the talk our men have heard, we have had to say to our troops, through their officers, that we come over to brace up the Allies and help them win and that they must pay no attention to loose remarks along that line by our Allied comrades.

The fact is that our officers and men are far and away superior to the tired European. High officers of the Allies have often dropped derogatory remarks about our poorly trained staff and high commanders, which our men have stood as long as they can. Even Mr. Tardieu [Official U.S. French liaison officer] said some of these things to me a few days ago. I replied, in rather forcible language, that we had now been patronized as long as we would stand for it, and I wished to hear no more of that sort of nonsense. Orders have been given by the French that all of our troops in sectors with the French would be

20. Pershing, *op. cit.*, 174.

King George V was "hands-on" during the War, seeking to put American troops under British command. Here he inspects members of the South Africa Native Labour Corps.

placed under our own officers and that American division commanders would be given command of their own sectors. This has come about since my insistence forced the French to agree to the formation of an American Field Army....[21]

The British did not like this at all and began to sabotage it. King George even came and made a personal appeal for more American troops to be assigned to the British command so that the "English-speaking peoples" could fight side by side and become permanent allies after the war.

While saying he agreed "friendly relations ought to be stronger after the war," Pershing was unmoved, and politely said that now that the United States was forming its own army, it would require all of its troops and that he "could make no promises."

The British still wanted U.S. troops to serve under British command. Both Marshall Haig and Lloyd George schemed behind Pershing's back to break the idea of an American Army, even encouraging Italy to make the absurd request for no less than 25 divisions, which of course came to nothing.

Commenting on these schemes, Pershing wrote in his war memoirs, "The impression left on our minds was, first, that the British desired to discourage the con-

centration of our forces into one army, and second, that perhaps there was a desire to check the growth of too-friendly relations between Americans and French." Besides he also wrote, "Our experience with the British had shown that, due to differences in national characteristics and military systems, the instruction and training of our troops by them retarded our progress."

The British used other forms of pressure. Knowing the United States was dependent on British shipping, in August 1918 the British began reducing the amount of shipping available to transport U.S. military supplies and men. The United States was still deficient in artillery, tanks, and aircraft, and therefore dependent on France and Britain to fill these gaps.

Unable to stop the formation of an Army, the British moved to prevent Pershing from carrying out his plans for a breakthrough on the St. Mihiel Front at Metz that would bring the war directly onto German territory.

Throughout the second half of August Pershing completed the organization of the First Army and even took command of the St. Mihiel front. Yet on August 30, within hours of taking control of the front, and only a matter of days before the American offensive in the sector was to begin, Marshall Foch came to Pershing's headquarters with an entirely new plan which was obviously drawn up in cooperation with, if not at the instigation of, the British. The plan called for nothing less than shifting the main area of Allied offensive activity fur-

---

21. *Ibid.*, 188.

ther to the West in front of Sedan, that would be launched in conjunction with a British offensive even further to the West, which is reality would be hundreds of kilometers from German territory. Foch proposed nothing less than breaking up the First Army and parcelling out its divisions among the French and the British. Pershing saw this as a transparent attempt to force the United States into a totally subordinate role in what was to prove to be the last offensive of the war, where France and Great Britain could be seen as having "won" the war, relegating to US to the role of their "native" auxiliaries. Thus, having only a secondary role in winning the war, the United States could only expect a secondary role in determining the peace.

For the sake of brevity, let it be said this meeting was so tense that it almost became the moral equivalent of a brawl. In the end, following another Allied conference on Sept 2nd, it was decided that the First Army would stay intact. It would carry out an attack on the St. Mihiel salient with the limited objective confined only to its reduction. The First Army would then be assigned to the Meuse-Argonne to the west of St. Mihiel, serving as the right flank of a combined attack in the direction of Sedan.

Except for having won the fight for an independent U.S. Army on its own front, Pershing was by no means pleased with this outcome, but he really had little choice under the circumstances. He managed not only to retain the First Army, but was able to form a Second Army. As we will see, MacArthur would confirm Pershing's original conception of the potential for a decisive breakthrough at Metz.

St. Mihiel: the Americans Demonstrate What Open Warfare Is

Demonstrating the contrast between the slaughter in the trenches, versus the American system of "open warfare," Pershing made the following observation when he took command of the St. Mihiel sector from his French counterpart:

When we arrived, the French General who was being relieved and his Chief of Staff, all dressed up in their red trousers and blue coats, came formally to turn over the command. The Chief of Staff carried two large volumes, each consisting of about 150 pages, the first being the Offensive Plan and the second the Defensive Plan for the St. Mihiel salient. These were presented to me

with considerable ceremony. My orders had already been prepared, the one for the attack comprising six pages, and the one for the defense eight pages. This incident is cited merely to show the difference between planning for trench warfare, to which the French were inclined, and open warfare, which we expected to conduct.[22]

On September 5 Pershing made the same point when he issued his "Combat Instructions" to the American First Army:

From a tactical point of view, the method of combat in trench warfare presents a marked contrast to that employed in open warfare, and the attempt by assaulting infantry to use trench warfare methods in an open warfare combat will be successful only at great cost. Trench warfare is marked by uniform formations, the regulation of space and time by higher commands down to the smallest details... fixed distances and intervals between units and individuals...little initiative... Open warfare is marked by irregularity of formations, comparatively little regulation of space and time by higher commanders, the greatest possible use of the infantry's own fire power to enable it to get forward... brief order and the greatest possible use of individual initiative by all troops engaged in the action...The infantry commander must oppose machine guns by fire from his rifles, his automatics and his rifle grenades and must close with the crews under cover of this fire and of ground beyond their flanks... The success of every unit from the platoon to the division must be exploited to the fullest extent. Where strong resistance is encountered, reenforcements must not be thrown in to make a frontal attack at this point, but must be pushed through gaps created by successful units, to attack these strong points in the flank of rear.[23]

Commenting on his plan, Pershing wrote:

[In] our original plans it had been my purpose after crushing the salient to continue the offensive through the Hindenburg Line and as much

22. *Ibid.*, 238.
23. *Ibid,*. 358.

farther as possible, depending upon the success attained and the opposition that developed.

As we have seen, however, the agreement reached in conference on Sept. 2nd limited the operations to the reduction of the salient itself. The basic features of the plan were not altered, but its objectives were defined and the number of troops to be employed was reduced.

Tactical surprise was essential to success, as the strength of the position would permit small forces of the enemy to inflict heavy losses on attacking troops. The sector had been quiet for some time and was usually occupied by seven enemy divisions in the front line, with two in reserve. It was estimated that the enemy could reinforce it by two divisions in two days, two more in three days, and as many divisions as were available in four days.

From captured documents and other sources of information, it seemed reasonable to conclude that the enemy had prepared a plan for withdrawal from the salient to the Hindenburg line in case of heavy Allied pressure. There was no doubt he was aware that an American attack was impending. Therefore, it was possible that he might increase his strength on our front....[24]

He then made this point, which would be key to MacArthur's mission in this two-front battle:

In that case, our task would be more difficult and as anything short of complete success would undoubtedly be seized upon to our disadvantage by those of the Allies who opposed the policy of forming an American army, no chances of a repulse in our first battle could be taken. These considerations prompted the decision to use some of our most experienced divisions along with the others.[25]

The order of battle for the main attack on the St. Mihiel salient was to be carried out by three American Corps. The I corps on the right with the 82nd Division

creative commons

The result of the trench warfare methods of the British-French command: mass graves throughout France. Here, the Roeselare French Military Cemetery.

astride the Moselle and the 90th, the 5th and the 2nd in order from east to west. Then came the IV Corps with the 89th, the 42nd and the 1st divisons. Here was to be the main attack, with the 42nd making the main effort. Then came the 5th Corps with the 26th, part of the 4th division, assisted by the French 15th Colonial Division, which was to conduct the secondary attack against the western face. The 26th alone was to make a deep advance, directed to the southeast toward Vigneulles.

At the point of the salient was the French II Colonial Corps, composed of three divisions.

The three American Corps comprised a total of nine divisions in the front line. Recall that American divisions, and therefore their corps, were twice the size in manpower of those of the French.

This was to be a battle of movement, not the typical "trench" warfare offensive that so constantly failed to achieve a breakthrough. In the typical trench warfare tactic an artillery barrage could last up to four days. This was supposedly needed to break up the barbed wire entanglements as well as strong points. In reality, it gave away any element of surprise, allowing the enemy time to bring up reinforcements and adjust his position in preparation for the attack. It also chewed up the no-mans land so much, that it became almost as impassable as the barbed wire.

By contrast, Pershing planned a preliminary barrage of no more than four hours. Left with no heavy tanks, because the British refused to give them for this battle,

24. *Ibid.*
25. *Ibid.*, 263.

National Archives

American engineers returning from the St. Mihiel front, after MacArthur was ordered not to proceed to the capture of Metz.

the plan was to have the engineers using special equipment move with the troops to cut paths through the barbed wire. They also threw chicken wire over the barbed wire, thereby allowing the men simply to walk over it. This facilitated rapid advance and a battle of maneuver, which totally amazed the French.

The battle started on September 12. The rapid advance of the Americans, who attacked within only a few hours of the artillery preparations, and simply walked over or through paths cut through the barbed wire, overwhelmed the enemy, who were forced into a disorganized retreat over open ground. By the 13th, days ahead of plans, Pershing and Pétain were in St. Mihiel and the salient was no more.

MacArthur Gets His Orders

As commander of the 84th brigade of the 42nd Division, MacArthur received his orders on September 10th. They were to be in their assigned position by September 12. "The 42nd division will attack in the center and deliver the main blow.... The division will seize its objective of the first phase, first day, without regard to the progress of neighboring divisions."[26]

In the early hours of September 12, after artillery preparation, MacArthur led his assault line forward,

which was followed by a squadron of light tanks led by Major George S. Patton, but the tanks soon bogged down in the mud. Commenting on the tactics he deployed, MacArthur wrote:

I have fought the German long enough to know his technique of defense. He concentrated to protect his center, but left his flanks weak. The field of action, the Bois de la Sonnard, lends itself to maneuver and we were able with little loss to pierce both flanks, envelop his center, and send his whole line into hurried retreat. By night fall we had the village of Essey and were out in the open in the broad plain of Woëvre, on the far side of which was the fortress of Metz, a stronghold since the days of Caesar.[27]

With these tactics, MacArthur's brigade advanced rapidly; in fact, the entire offensive operation made exceedingly rapid progress out of all expectation of the Allies, although not of the Americans, who had in fact expected this rapid advance. MacArthur's brigade advanced the most rapidly and soon found itself in front of Metz. In his *Reminiscences* MacArthur observed:

...As I had suspected Metz was practically defenseless at that moment. Its combat garrison had been temporarily withdrawn to support other sectors of action. Here was an unparalleled opportunity to break the Hindenburg line at its pivotal point. There it lay, our prize wide open for the taking. Take it and we would be in an excellent position to cut off south Germany from the rest of the country; it would lead to the invasion of central Germany by way of the practically undefended Moselle Valley. Victory at Metz would cut the great lines of communication and supply behind the German front, and might bring the war to a quick close.

I recommended as forcefully as I could that my brigade immediately attack the town, promising that I would be in its famous city hall by

---

26. Amerine, William Henry, *Alabama's Own in France* (New York: Eaton & Gettinger, 1919), 170-171.

27. MacArthur, *op.cit.* 70-71.

nightfall. I emphasized that the tactical success of the last days meant that little in itself unless fully exploited, that to tie us down now would be 'like a cavalry horse on a lariat tied to a picket fence. It can go so far and not farther, no matter how much richer the grass is beyond its reach.' Division, Corps, and Army agreed with me [This included Pershing since he was Army commander], but the high command [the Allied command] disapproved. Other plans had been made—the Meuse-Argonne drive—and while my ideas were deeply appreciated, no change would be made. I have always thought this was one of the great mistakes of the war. Had we seized this unexpected opportunity we would have saved thousands of American lives lost in the dim recesses of the Argonne Forest. It was an example of the inflexibility in pursuit of previously conceived ideas that is, unfortunately, too frequent in modern warfare. Final decisions are made not at the front by those who are there, but many miles away by those who can but guess at the possibilities. The essence of victory lies in the answer to where and when.

The enemy lost no time. He brought up thousands of troops from Strasbourg and other sectors, and within a week the whole Allied army could not have stormed Metz....[28]

In an indirect reference to MacArthur's own observations, Pershing writes:

Reports received on the 13th and 14th indicated that the enemy was retreating in considerable disorder. Without doubt, an immediate continuation of the advance would have carried us well beyond the Hindenburg Line and possibly into Metz, and the temptation to press on was very great, but we would probably have become involved and delayed the greater Meuse-Argonne operation, to which we were wholly committed.[29]

Describing the rest of his role in this battle MacArthur wrote, "I was directed to organize a line of defense and I established my headquarters in the Chateau at St. Benoit. I was promptly shelled out. In order to confuse the enemy, I was ordered to stage, on the night of September 25, a powerful double raid against the center of his line to make him think we were about to resume our advance, whereas the real attack was to be in the Argonne.

"The raid was to be made on two German strong points, one a fortified farm—which in France meant a group of buildings with walls connecting them—and the other a village of stone buildings with trenches and strong barbed wire entanglements..." MacArthur ordered an artillery barrage, "The fire from these ninety guns was so accurate and so overwhelming that both Germany garrisons were practically annihilated. I maneuvered the infantry carefully so as to make a lot of noise and much display, but not to bring it into the line of fire. I actually lost fewer than twenty men killed and wounded. Shortly afterward, the division was relieved and went into preparation for what became the final drive of the war. I was cited for the St. Benoit actions— my sixth Silver Star."

MacArthur's 8,000-man brigade captured 10,000 prisoners.

The tremendous success of this operaton prompted Marshall Pétain to issue the following order to his own troops after the battle:

It is desirable for a certain number of French officers, non-commissioned officers and soldiers to visit the terrain so that they can fully understand the manner in which the American infantry has been able, during the last attacks carried out by the American First Army, to overcome the obstacles encountered during the advance and not destroyed by artillery or by tanks.

The American units have cut themselves a passage with wire-cutters through the thick bands of wire or they have walked over these wire entanglements with much skill, rapidity, and decision. It is interesting that our infantry soldiers should see for themselves the nature of the difficulties thus overcome and that they should persuade themselves that they also are capable of doing as much on occasion.

The Meuse-Argonne Meatgrinder

The new front put the American right flank on the Meuse river and its left flank to the west on the Argonne Forest along an 80-mile front. "A million American soldiers," MacArthur wrote, "were to attempt a break-

28. *Ibid.*
29. Pershing, *op. cit.*, 270.

American gunners in Argonne Forest, September 1918.

National Archives and Records Administration

through in the center of the Western Front to Sedan, a breakthrough which would mean the collapse of the powerful Hindenburg Line and the defeat of Germany."[30]

Behind this front on the line Metz-Sedan lay the intersection of the great rail network the Germans had developed that would bring supplies from the direction of Cologne-Liege-Namur, then south to Sedan, and from Koblenz down the Moselle valley to Metz, from which the entire front to the west was supplied. This defined this front as the most decisive of this last offensive of the war.

On the other hand it was the most difficult terrain along the entire front. MacArthur wrote, "In 1914, when the great German armies first marched to conquest, they had come through the Argonne, seized it and had never been dislodged. The terrain was so difficult, so easily defended, that the French had never attempted to attack. It was so powerfully fortified over four years that doubt existed in Allied high circles that any troops in the world could drive out the Germans. The Germans themselves boasted they would drown the American attack in its own blood."

Pershing's original plan, and MacArthur's later observations about making the decisive breakthrough at Metz, had been designed to outflank this front by breaking the Hindenburg line at Metz lying to the East. This would have enveloped Sedan from the east, behind the strong position of the Meuse-Argonne.

Pershing was well aware of this from the beginning.

One senses that the British and the French were aware of this as well, and maneuvered, pressured, and in the end forced the Americans to accept the limited objectives on the St. Mihiel-Metz front, and shift their effort to a front position on the Meuse-Argonne.

The British and the French seemed to have expected the United States to fail from the beginning, thinking that they could not logistically shift an entire army of 500,000 men in time to launch their attack. This feat was in fact carried out in time, to the total surprise of the Allies.

On September 26, on the first day of the offensive, the United States had advanced to and captured Montfaucon, an accomplishment that Pétain thought could not be finished before winter set in. The Germans nonetheless had carefully prepared a system of defenses through the sector, MacArthur wrote:

Into this red inferno the American had jumped off on September 26, and foot by foot, over scarred and wooded hill and valley, had fought their bloody way from trench to trench to the enemy's main line of resistance. The German, alive to the threat, had a machine-gun nest behind every rock, a cannon behind every natural embrasure. Here was the key sector of the famous Hindenburg Line, known as the Krunhilde Stallung [sic. It was in fact called the Kriemhilde Stellung]. Here was the last line of the mighty German defenses in the Argonne. Breach it and there would be laid bare Sedan and Mezieres, the two huge rail centers, through which all the German armies as far as the North Sea at Ostend were supplied. Take Sedan and every German army to the west would be outflanked. The railroads by which they could withdraw such large masses of troops would be either in American hands or under fire from American guns. It would mean the capture of troops running into the hundreds of thousands. It would mean the end of the war.[31]

---

30. MacArthur, *op. cit.*, 73.

31. *Ibid.*

The 42nd was not in the first wave of the attack, but was thrown in at the crucial point where the entire offensive was being held up at a point called the Côte de Châtillon, where the American First Division, after driving a deep salient into the German front, was stopped. The Côte de Châtillon was a high point that jutted out forming a natural bastion along the German front. As MacArthur wrote, "This salient was dominated by the Côte de Châtillon stronghold which raked the Allied flank and thus stopped the advancing American attack. Every effort to go forward had been stopped cold by this flanking fire."

"I carefully reconnoitered the desolate and forbidding terrain that confronted my brigade. There were rolling hills, heavily wooded valleys of death between the endless folds of ridges.... I saw at once that the previous advances had failed because it had not been recognized that the Côte de Châtillon was the keystone of the whole German position; that until it was captured we would be unable to advance. I proposed to capture the Côte de Châtillon by concentrating troops on it, instead of continuing to spread the troops along a demonstratedly unsuccessful line of attack. Both the division and corps commanders approved."

Then there was the famous demand by the V Corps Commander and former associate of Arthur MacArthur, General Charles P. Summerall, who said, "Give me Châtillon, or give me a list of five thousand casualties." To which MacArthur said he would take it "or my name will be head of the list."

The front of MacArthur's 84th Brigade lay astride the Côte de Châtillon, which protruded into the 84th sector with a broad front which tapered back on the sides. As MacArthur explains, he would deploy his 168th regiment on the right, and the 167th on the left. Knowing that the Germans maintain a strong center while keeping their flanks weak, his purpose was to launch a pincer operation with the 168th attacking up the right flank of the Châtillon and the 167th up the left. MacArthur wrote that during a reconnaissance of the Châtillon, he "discovered that, as usual, while the German center, where the 1st Division had spent its blood, seemed impregnable, the flanks were vulnera-

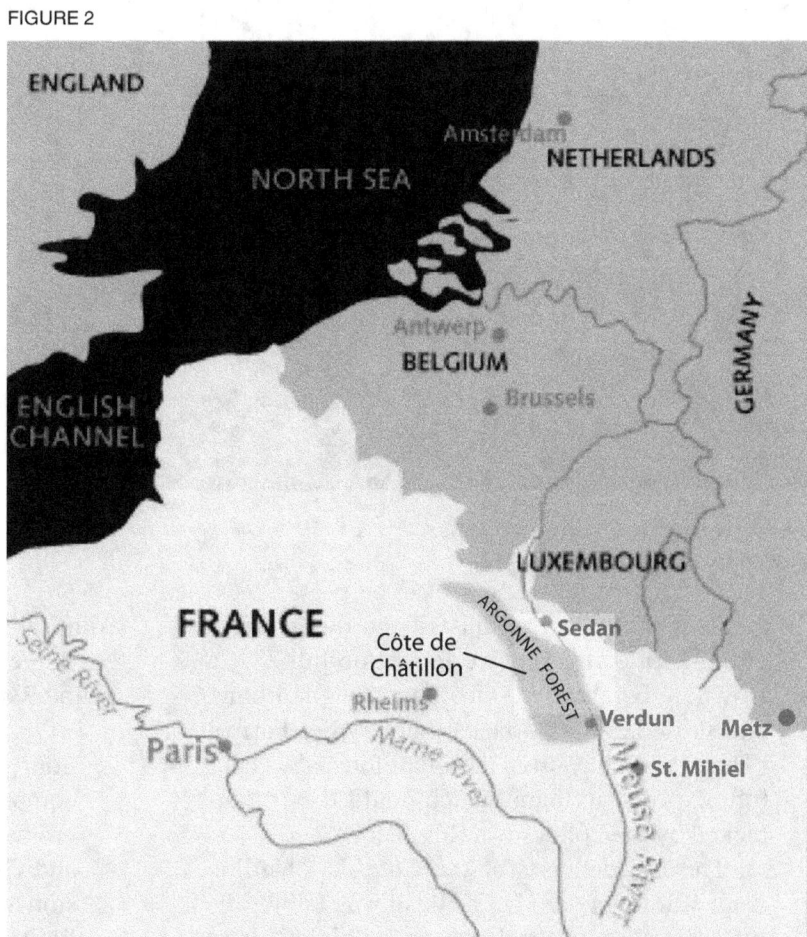

FIGURE 2

The lay of the land during the battle for the Argonne.

ble. His deep belt of entanglement and trench dribbled out at the ends. There was where I planned to strike with my Alabama cotton growers (the 167th Regiment) on the left, my Iowa farmers (168th Regiment) on the right. I planned to use every machine gun and artillery piece as covering fire."

This was harder than it may sound, because those flanks were also covered by other hills which had first to be taken before the Châtillon itself could be attacked.

We moved out in the misty dawn, and from then on little units of our men crawled and sneaked and side slipped forward from one bit of cover to another. When the chance came we would close in suddenly to form squads or platoons for a swift envelopment that would gain a toehold on some slope or deadly hillock. Death, cold and remorseless, whistled and sung its way through our ranks, but by nightfall Hill 288 was in Iowa

The signing of the Treaty of Versailles, June 28, 1919, the signal for the beginning of the next war.

hands. That night I readjusted and reorganized, and the following day we fought up hill 282, a frowning height of 900 feet, and fought around and skirted hill 205 to take the Tuileries Ferme. (This was on the left of the Châtillon and its capture exposed its flank which could then be attacked by the 168th Iowa Regiment.)

The last defenses of the Côte de Châtillon were still before us, but as dusk was falling the First Battalion of the 168th under Major Lloyd Ross moved from the right while a battalion of the 167th under Major Ravee Norris stalked stealthily from the left toward the gap in the wire. The two battalions, like the arms of a relentless pincer, closed in from both sides. Officers fell and sergeants leaped to the command. Companies dwindled to platoons and corporals took over. At the end, Major Ross had only 300 men and 6 officers left of 1,450 men and 25 officers. That is the way the Côte de Châtillon fell, and that is the ways those gallant citizen soldiers, so far from home, won the approach to victory.

Both his divisional commander and Summerall recommended MacArthur for the Medal of Honor and a promotion. Both were turned down; nonetheless, to his satisfaction MacArthur was awarded another Distinguished Service Cross.

While this broke the strongest point of the line and broke the back of the Germans, nonetheless the hard fight continued for the next three weeks to the end of the war on November 11th. In the last days it was said that Pershing wanted the U.S. soldiers to be the first in Sedan, the site of France's ignoble defeat in the Franco-Prussian war in 1871. He ordered his divisions to race to its capture. In the haste of battle divisional boundaries were crossed, which led to MacArthur's capture "by friendly forces" from another division who took him for a German. He was soon released, and the war was soon over.

While the Germans were clearly defeated, that "second front," the British-dominated Entente, was not.

In November 1918, only a few days after the signing of the Armistice, the U.S. Navy's London Planning Section, which was headed by the reputedly anglophile Admiral Sims, nonetheless warned that Britain could target the United States. An estimate written at the time by the Planning Section stated:

> Four great Powers have arisen in the world to compete with Great Britain for commercial supremacy on the seas—Spain, Holland, France and Germany. Each of these Powers in succession have been defeated by Great Britain and her fugitive Allies. A fifth commercial Power, the greatest one yet, is now arising to compete for at least commercial equality with Great Britain. Already the signs of jealousy are visible. Historical precedent warns us to watch closely the moves we make or permit to be made.[32]

At the end of the war, the prestige of the United States and its army was enormous in the eyes of public opinion in Europe, a fact that enraged the British, who redoubled their efforts to prevent the United States from imposing a settlement in Europe that would assure a peace for the future. Unfortunately they had a willing accomplice in the person of "colonel" Edward House and his dupe President Woodrow Wilson. By the end of 1919, the world was already sliding on a course that would lead to the next war, and the U.S. Navy and Army began work on War Plan Red, a contingency plan if war broke out with Great Britain.

32. Herwig, Holger H., *The United States in German Naval Planning 1889-1941* (Little Brown, 1976), 171.

Silk Road Universities Network Founded at Korean Conference

Aug. 30—The following speeches, by the founder of the international Schiller Institutes, Helga Zepp-LaRouche, and by *EIR* Asia analyst Mike Billington, were presented on Aug. 22 in Gyeongju, South Korea, at the inaugural conference of the "Silk Road Universities Network (SUN)."

Representatives of 43 universities and organizations from 22 countries along the land and maritime Silk Roads participated in the conference, sponsored by Hankuk University of Foreign Studies with national and local government support.

Gyeongju itself, the ancient capital of Korea and a major port on the ancient maritime Silk Road, organized a months-long cultural and educational exposition on the Silk Road. South Korean President Park Geun-hye, who is from South Gyeongsang Province (the province of Gyeongju), and the governor of Gyeonsang Kim Kwan-yong, have promoted the Silk Road campaign in South Korea and its outreach to all the countries along the land and sea Silk Roads.

The SUN organization was founded with the intention, as stated in its Articles of Association, of "restoring 'Silkroadia,' the Silk Road Spirit—a symbol of the bridge between East and West by banding together universities located on the land and sea routes of the Silk Road and contributing to world peace and the creative development of civilization by training future leaders devoted to the spirit."

The Founding Declaration, adopted by the members attending the inaugural conference, addressed the urgency of the development process embedded in Silkroadia to end the devolving strategic crisis facing the Eurasian continent:

Sadly, however, we are witnessing terrible murder and destruction in some regions along the Silk Road today. They have become the ground on which nations fight wars with each other, and where cultures and religions clash in

The Silk Road

dispute. If we allow these conflicts to continue they will escalate and darken the future of the Silk Road, diminishing this great source of pride into a place of shame and agony.

The Declaration states that overcoming this crisis of civilization requires a "genuine appreciation for individual differences and universal truths," calling on the intellectuals and universities gathered in the SUN to adopt the "responsibility to resolve" these existential threats to civilization.

The speeches below, presented by Helga Zepp-LaRouche and Mike Billington, emphasized that the new institution must go beyond the academic mission, to intervene internationally with the Silk Road perspective, on a global rather than only Eurasian scale, providing the necessary policy alternative to the extreme danger of global warfare now facing civilization from the United States and NATO geopolitical confrontation with Russia and China, as the western financial system collapses into chaos.

The first panel of the conference, dedicated to the subject "The Future of the Silk Road," was to be chaired by Mrs. LaRouche. However, due to her inability to attend the conference in person, Mike Billington chaired the panel and read her speech, as well as his own.

A New Era of Mankind Where We Become Truly Human

by Helga Zepp-LaRouche

This is the text of the presentation by Helga Zepp-La-Rouche to the 2015 Silk-Road International Academic Conference—How to Establish Silk-Road Studies as an Independent Discipline of Research—in Gyeongju, South Korea, the ancient capital of Korea, on Aug. 21. The accompanying slides were shown with the presentation.

Presentation for the panel "Future Vision of the Silk Road"

When we are talking about the New Silk Road as a vision for the future, we should see it as a synonym not only for a new just economic order, and emphatically as the basis for a peace order for the Twenty-first Century, based on completely different economic and scientific principles than the previous system of globalization, but also as a new paradigm concerning the identity of the human species as the only creative species known so far in the universe.

Concerning the first aspect, in respect to the new economic system, tremendous progress has been made with the recent BRICS and Shanghai Cooperation Organization (SCO) summits. In these meetings, the integration of the Eurasian Economic Union and the Silk Road Economic Belt Policy, as well as the Shanghai Cooperation Organization (SCO) transport system, were agreed upon, which will bring tremendous benefits to all peoples of Eurasia. Through new banking arrangements, such as those of the Asian Infrastructure Bank, the New Development Bank, the SCO Bank, the South Asia Association for Regional Cooperation Bank, the New Silk Road Fund, the Maritime Silk Road Fund, and the BRICS Contingency Reserve Arrangement,—all devoted to investments in the real economy and to fight off speculation,—a completely new economic and financial order has gotten well underway, which, in terms of human and natural resources and potential,

Slide 1

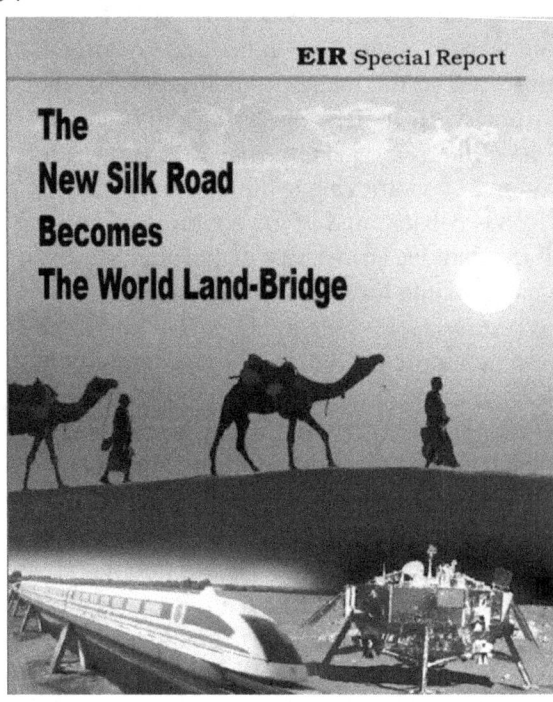

represents the locomotive of the future world economy. (**See Slide 1**)

Both President Putin and President Xi Jinping, have emphasized that, while the BRICS is an organization of its own, they are open to collaboration with all other nations, including the United States, as well as European and Asian countries. President Xi Jinping has called this an all-inclusive "win-win" policy, in which all participating nations will enjoy mutual benefits. President Putin has reiterated that openness. The concept of the New Silk Road is therefore the most important strategic initiative, because it is the only available policy on the table to overcome the idea of geopolitics, which was the basis for the two World Wars in the Twentieth Century.

The prospect that nations, or a group of nations,

would have legitimate geopolitical interests which would pit them against each other, must be replaced with the idea that there is a higher level of reason, on which historical, ethnic, or other conflicts disappear. Mankind must be defined in this way, for the first time in its history, by the common aims of the human species.

From Financial Crisis to War

This is not some vision for the far-distant future, but it is the indispensable basis for an immediate intervention into the strategic situation today, because there is an acute danger of a blowout of the trans-Atlantic financial system which would be much more dangerous than the collapse of Lehman Brothers and AIG in September 2008. Directly related to that, is the danger of the escalation of the confrontation between NATO, and Russia and China, into what could become a global thermonuclear war.

"Doomsday Clock for Global Market Crash Strikes One Minute to Midnight as Central Banks Lose Control," was one headline in the British *Daily Telegraph* on August 18th, being symptomatic of a general recognition among financial analysts that today there exist all the markers of the situation before the crash in September 2008. But today the too-big-to-fail banks are an average of 40% larger, their derivative exposure is around 80% bigger, and the so-called tool box of the central banks is empty, since the interest rates are already at about zero percent, and quantitative easing has been going on for many years, without getting the real economy restarted.

It is that pending systemic collapse of the trans-Atlantic financial system which is the acute basis for the danger that the West will indeed step into the much discussed Thucydides trap right now, resulting from the same geopolitical reasons, described by the authors of the geopolical doctrine, Halford Mackinder and Alfred Milner, before World War I. That same impulse very much governs those who wishfully call Russia only a regional power, which is ludicrous in light of Russia's upgraded strategic nuclear capacities, or those who see in the rise of China something which must be contained.

The European Leadership Network, ELN, a think-tank consisting of former European and Russian defense ministers, just issued a stern warning that the presently ongoing maneuvers by NATO and Russia are making a war in Europe more likely. "Russia prepares for a war against NATO, and NATO prepares for a confrontation against Russia," the study writes. Such a war,

however, would not be limited to Europe; it lies in the nature of nuclear weapons, that once they are used, the conflict will become a global thermonuclear war, which would in all likelihood lead to the annihilation of the human species.

War Avoidance Through Development

In order to prevent that, it is urgent that the New Silk Road perpective be put even more energetically on the international agenda as a war-avoidance policy.

The Schiller Institute last year presented a 370-Page scientific study entitled *The New Silk Road Becomes the World Land Bridge*, which is the outline for an infrastructural integration of all continents, through a comprehensive system of fast train systems, highways, waterways, tunnels, and bridges as the arteries for development corridors. This comprehensive plan for the reconstuction of the world economy would provide enormous advantages for each participating country, enabling every part of the planet to participate in a "win-win" perspective. (**See Slide 2**)

This will be the way to bring to the landlocked areas of the planet the same advantages which previously only characterized areas located on oceans or rivers. This infrastructure will not only be the precondition for the development of industry and agriculture, but especially for the increase of the productivity of the respective populations. As the opening-up of previously undeveloped areas progresses, and the industrialization intensifies, the speed and connectivity of transport becomes more important, and therefore the advantages of fast train systems over land become more significant than the cheaper transport by ships. Rather than transporting crude raw materials over many weeks over the oceans, where nothing is happening with them, countries can process them in industrial centers with a highly differentiated division of labor and complex subsequent processing. Time is of the essence.

One big area of the planet where a solution urgently must be found is obviously Southwest Asia and large parts of northern and central Africa. These large regions have been almost totally destroyed through wars, which were motivated by lies, and where the so-called war on terrorism has generated more terrorists with each bomb, drone, or killing. If the entire region from the Caucasus to the Persian Gulf and the Arabian Sea, from Afghanistan to the Mediterranean, as well as the just-mentioned parts of Africa, which literally have been bombed back to the Stone Age, is going to have a chance to cease to

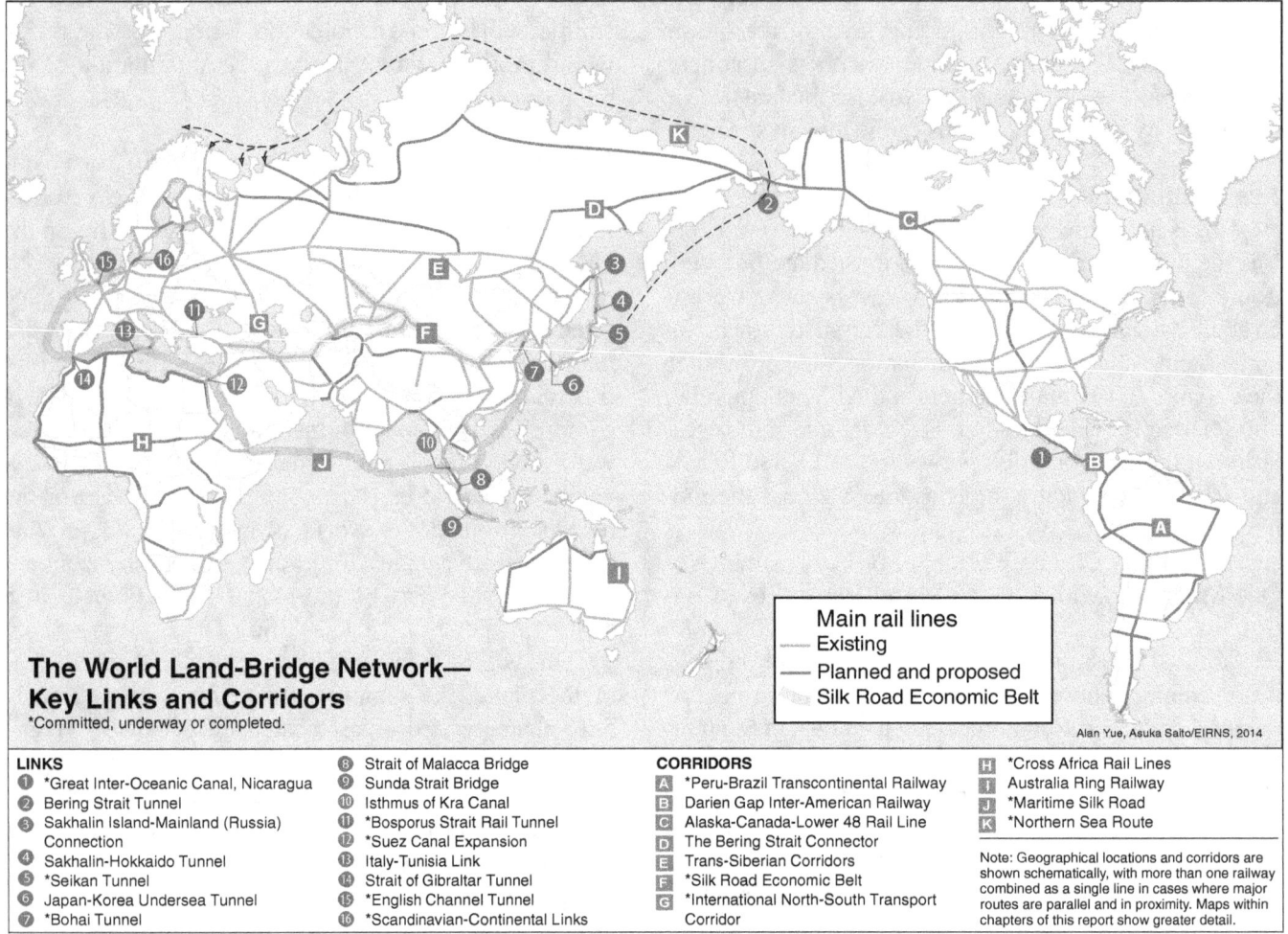

**The World Land-Bridge Network—
Key Links and Corridors**
*Committed, underway or completed.

Main rail lines
--- Existing
— Planned and proposed
Silk Road Economic Belt

Alan Yue, Asuka Saito/EIRNS, 2014

LINKS
1. *Great Inter-Oceanic Canal, Nicaragua
2. Bering Strait Tunnel
3. Sakhalin Island-Mainland (Russia) Connection
4. *Sakhalin-Hokkaido Tunnel
5. *Seikan Tunnel
6. Japan-Korea Undersea Tunnel
7. *Bohai Tunnel
8. Strait of Malacca Bridge
9. Sunda Strait Bridge
10. Isthmus of Kra Canal
11. *Bosporus Strait Rail Tunnel
12. *Suez Canal Expansion
13. Italy-Tunisia Link
14. Strait of Gibraltar Tunnel
15. *English Channel Tunnel
16. *Scandinavian-Continental Links

CORRIDORS
A. *Peru-Brazil Transcontinental Railway
B. Darien Gap Inter-American Railway
C. Alaska-Canada-Lower 48 Rail Line
D. The Bering Strait Connector
E. Trans-Siberian Corridors
F. *Silk Road Economic Belt
G. *International North-South Transport Corridor
H. *Cross Africa Rail Lines
I. Australia Ring Railway
J. *Maritime Silk Road
K. *Northern Sea Route

Note: Geographical locations and corridors are shown schematically, with more than one railway combined as a single line in cases where major routes are parallel and in proximity. Maps within chapters of this report show greater detail.

be a breeding ground for ever more barbaric forms of terrorism, there must be a real development perspective. (**See Slide 3**)

Right now the refugee crisis erupting out of both Southwest Asia as well as Central and North Africa, is of a dimension not seen since the end of World War II when people fled from Eastern into Western Europe. At that time, 12 million people fled devastation.

Today, according to UN figures, there are 60 million people on the march, most of them being harbored in poor, completely overstretched neighboring countries, with a very large portion trying to somehow get into Europe. There, many of the communities are already overstretched, and in the short term, social explosions and xenophobic backlashes are threatening the stability of the societies.

Especially in light of the recent revelations of the former U.S. DIA director General Michael Flynn con-

cerning the emergence of ISIS, it is urgent that an analysis of the root cause of the refugee crisis be conducted. But then a profound cure for the problem has to be offered.

Already, in 2012, we presented a comprehensive plan for the development of this region as a whole, at a conference of the Schiller Institute in Frankfurt. Only if all the region's big neighbors,—namely Russia, China, India, Pakistan, Iran, and Egypt, hopefully in cooperation with some European nations, such as Germany, France, and Italy, and the United States,—agree to, together with the BRICS, extend the New Silk Road development perspective into Southwest Asia and Africa, is there any possibility that the vision of a better future will convince especially the young men, that it is better to study to become a scientist or engineer and raise a family, rather than joining the growing number of jihadist groups. The perspective of a higher level of reason, embedded in the concept of the New Silk Road, the idea of peace through development, is the only way that the deep and bitter hostilities between different ethnic and religious groupings can be overcome.

What is needed is an integrated development program, including a war against the desert with the development of huge new water sources, infrastructure, industry, agriculture, new smart cities, and science and research centers. **(See Slide 4)** If all the countries which are presently threatened by the terrorism emanating from that region, would collaborate in this development, the danger could be overcome.

Likewise, rather than upgrading the border defenses with Frontex[1] and deploying gun boats against streams of hundreds of thousands—potentially millions—of refugees, who are fleeing from war, hunger and disease, taking a 50% risk of death by trying to cross the Mediterranean, would it not make more sense to develop these regions, so that people would rather stay in their home countries, than go into a horribly uncertain future? We have to make up our minds what kind of condition that part of the world should be in, 50-100 years from now; in a miserable dark age at best, or in modern times with a decent living for everybody.

Due to climate change, caused primarily by solar and galactic influences on planet Earth, the belt of deserts, ranging from the Atlantic coast of Africa all the way through the Sahara and Sahel, the Arabian peninsula, the Near and Middle East to China, is expanding presently in a similar fashion to the desert spreading in the Southwest of the United States, and parts of Central and South America. The obvious answer to this problem is the creation of large amounts of fresh water through a variety of methods, such as desalination of large amounts of

Slide 3

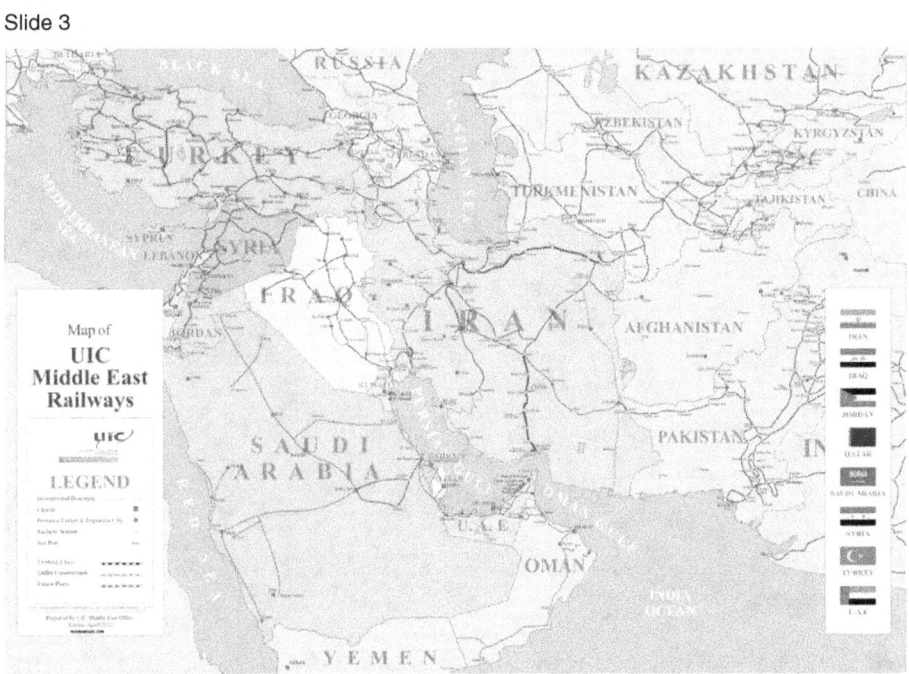

Slide 4

ocean water through nuclear energy, continental water diversification and management projects, weather modification, and ionization of atmospheric moisture.

In several countries, atmospheric ionization systems have been successfully used to increase precipitation, and in this way affect the associated weather processes. Successful application of this method, which imitates processes occurring naturally in our solar system and galaxy, has been tested over three decades. With international cooperation concerning the further development of these technologies, the desertification of the mentioned regions of the world could be combat-

---

1. Frontex is described as the agency of the European Union that manages the cooperation between national border guards that has undertaken to secure the external borders of the union, including from illegal immigration, human trafficking, and terrorist infiltration. The agency was established in 2004 and has its seat in Warsaw, Poland.

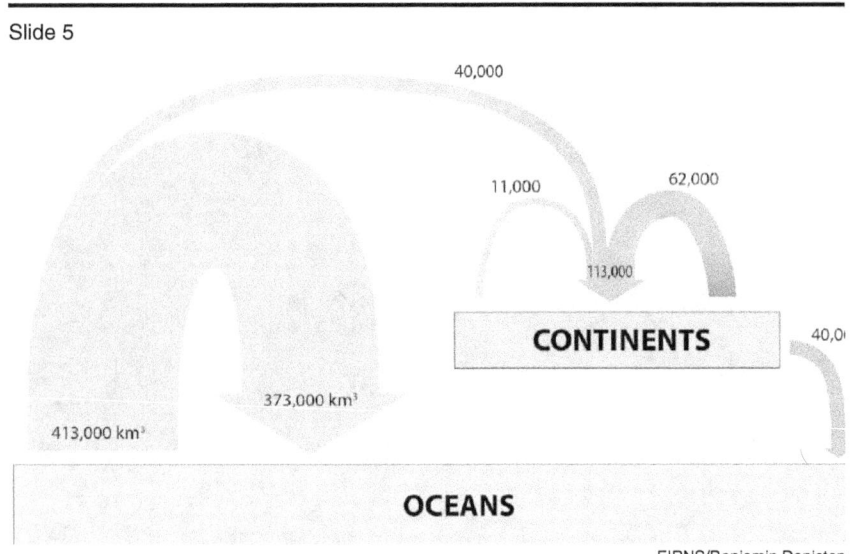

40,000

11,000   62,000

113,000

CONTINENTS   40,0

373,000 km³

413,000 km³

OCEANS

EIRNS/Benjamin Deniston

The abundance of water potentially available to Earth is readily discernible in this schematic of moisture flows.

ted in a completely new way: by the management of the water resources of the atmosphere! (**See Slide 5**)

Joint space research and travel is one of the foremost areas constituting the future common aims of mankind. It will lead to revolutionary and necessary insights into our Solar System and Galaxy. It is existential for protecting mankind from dangers from space, such as asteroids, meteoroids, and comets, and it will be absolutely essential to identify sources of practically limitless new resources, such as, for example, the mining of Helium 3 on the moon as a fuel for a future fusion economy on Earth. If one considers the enormous progress mankind has made scientifically and technologically, it is obvious that space science is presently still in its very first baby shoes.

At the recent BRICS Youth Summit meeting of youth representatives in Kazan, Russia, on July 8-9, the participants signed a memorandum of understanding, which urged the BRICS member-nations to set up a joint space station, as well as to commit to the creation of a system of research institutions, the development of technology parks, and the organization of exhibitions on research-related subjects, according to a news item issued on the Russian BRICS website. The MOU document stated: "Working together on a space station for exploring outer space and carrying out manned programs could become a symbol of the new world order based on BRICS values."

While the concept of the New Silk Road becoming the World Land Bridge completes the era of the infra-structural development of the planet Earth, the extension of the New Silk Road into space represents the comprehension of our planet as part of our Galaxy and will enable us to understand the galactic processes of which we are a part.

A New Renaissance

The beauty of our world is, that it has many rich cultures, which have contributed to the universal history of the human species. The ancient Silk Road not only led to an exchange of goods, such as silk, porcelain, glass, and spices, but it made possible the exchange of the most advanced technologies of that time, leading to the improvement of the living standard of all participating countries. With that came an exchange of cultures, philosophies, and new ideas, bringing human civilization forward. (**See Slide 6**)

The New Silk Road will make it possible for each culture on the planet to contribute its best and most noble expression in the areas of Classical music, poetry, the visual arts, philosophy, and science. There will be an exchange of the high phases of each culture and civilization; young and old people will study the Greek classical period, Confucianism, the Gupta period, the Abbasid era, the Andalusian renaissance, the Joseon [or Chosun] period, the golden Italian renaissance, the German classics, to only name a few.

By learning to know the best of each other's culture,

A statue of Chinese philosopher Confucius on the grounds of the Confucius Temple in Beijing

Scientist Albert Einstein playing his violin.

a deep understanding and even a love of the other cultures will develop, and in this way prejudices, chauvinism, and backwardness will be replaced by the spirit of a new renaissance, which will build on the knowledge of the old cultures, but will enlarge and enrich that wealth to the creation of new works of art in all fields.

The New Silk Road will open up a completely new paradigm for mankind, one in which that quality which differentiates human beings from all other species—their creative power of reason—will become the normal outlook. What was only characteristic in past history of exceptional individuals,—the great discoverers, scientists, composers, and poets,—can now become the more natural condition for more and more people, especially when each child has access to a universal education that emphasizes these treasures. This new renaissance will be the demonstration of the theory of the Russian scientist Vladimir Vernadsky, that in the evolution of the universe, the noösphere will increasingly influence and dominate the biosphere. The human species will develop its identity as the truly creative species. (**See Slide 7**)

So, we as humanity have reached the most important crossroads of our entire history. Either we can consciously organize our affairs based on the new paradigm which the New Silk Road represents, and deliberately create a new era in human history, or we may have the same fate as the dinosaurs. I would hope very much, that this conference and the New Silk Road study center will send a powerful message to the world to this effect. Thank you very much.

Peace Through Development— The Unity of East and West

by Michael O. Billington

My associate Helga Zepp-LaRouche, founder of the international Schiller Institutes, warned in her presentation to this conference that the world is threatened with global war, even thermonuclear war, for no legitimate reason. She emphasized that the combination of the New Silk Road initiative and the recent creation of new international financial institutions associated with the BRICS, the SCO, and others, aimed at facilitating large-scale infrastructure projects around the world, was the necessary precondition for cooperation among all the world's nations, including the western nations, towards meeting the common aims of mankind.

But we are living through perhaps the greatest crisis of the global financial system in modern history, with the trans-Atlantic financial system experiencing repeated convulsions, while governments choose to bail out huge quantities of speculative debt, and implement greater and greater levels of austerity on their populations, rather than reorganizing that debt in the manner carried out by Franklin Roosevelt in 1933: i.e., writing off the worthless speculative portion of that debt and directing new federal credit into real physical development and employment.

Many of these western leaders look at the development of the Silk Road and the new financial institutions centered in Asia not as an opportunity for cooperation, but as a threat to the West's access to the raw materials and labor power in the developing sector of the world, without providing the basic infrastructure required by these nations in return, as the Silk Road process does. This is the underlying conflict which is fueling the drive for war, which must be overcome.

Encircling the World

Pope Paul VI, in his 1967 Encyclical, *Populorum Progressio*, Development of Peoples, stated that "the new name for peace is development." In fact this is not really so new. Gottfried Leibniz, the great Seventeenth and Eighteenth Century philosopher and statesman who is properly considered the founder of the science of physical economy, in his journal *Novissima Sinica, News from China*, reporting to the European people on the extraordinary philosophic and social traditions and the economic developments taking place in China at that time, which were being conveyed to him by the Jesuit missionaries in China, said the following:

> I consider it a singular plan of the fates that human cultivation and refinement should today be concentrated, as it were, in the two extremes of our continent, in Europe and in China, which adorns the Orient as Europe does the opposite edge of the Earth. Perhaps Supreme Providence has ordained such an arrangement, so that, as the most cultivated and distant peoples stretch out their arms to each other, those in between may gradually be brought to a better way of life.

Is this not a perfect reflection of the noble purpose of the Silk Road today?

You can compare that to the British Empire apologist Rudyard Kipling, who famously said that "East is East and West is West, and never the twain shall meet." I would argue that this is not an observation, but a statement of policy intent, to keep the world divided.

In America, the concept of the "common aims of mankind" was the bedrock of our best leaders, who were unfortunately few and far between. Alexander Hamilton, our first Treasury Secretary, created national banking institutions not unlike the AIIB and the BRICS New Development Bank, based on extending federal credit for "internal improvements," the term at that time for infrastructure. The great Lafayette called America the "beacon of hope and the temple of liberty" for all mankind.

FIGURE 1
Trans-Greater Tumen Region Transport Corridors

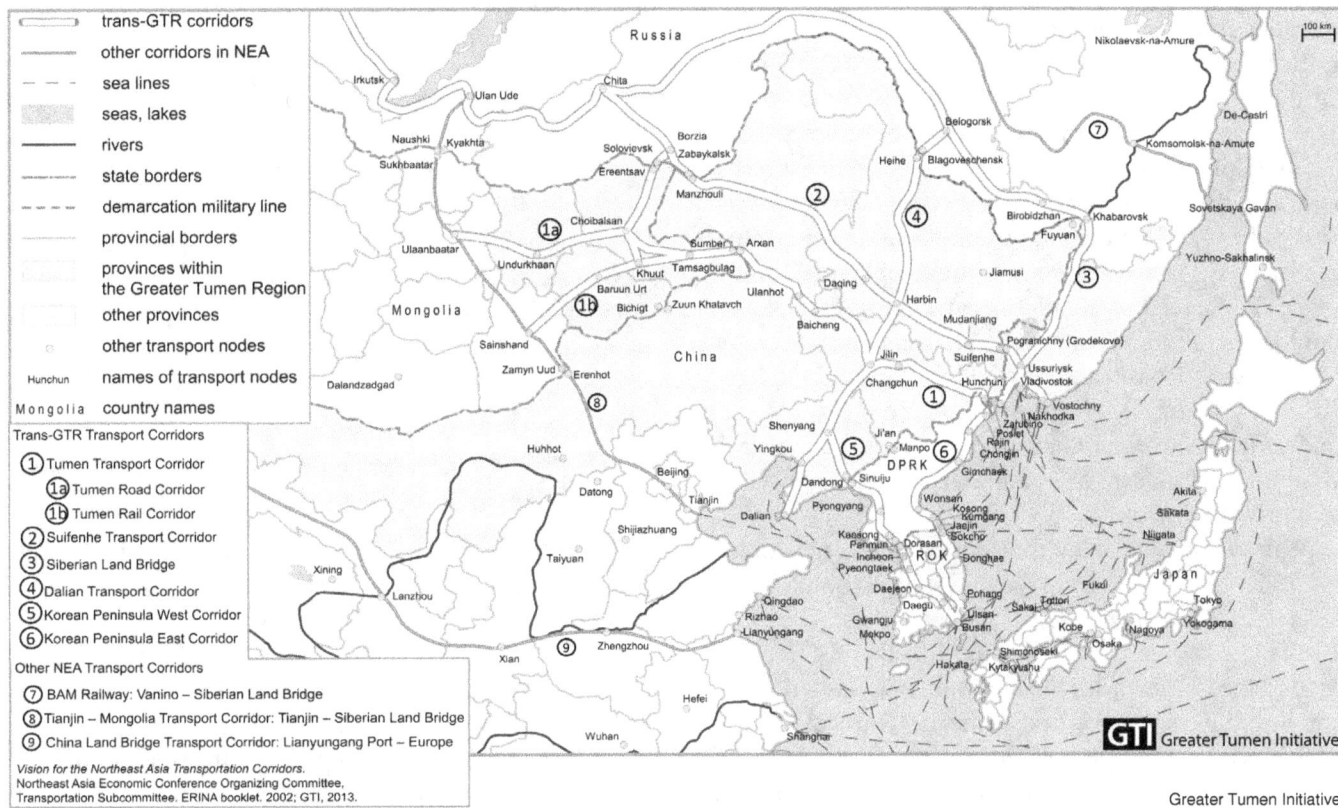

The development of the port of Rason (shown here as Rajin, in the northeast corner of North Korea) is paradigmatic of "peace through development," in this case through cooperation between China, Russia, South Korea, and North Korea.

In the time of Lincoln, while he was building the Trans-continental Railroad, linking the Atlantic and the Pacific by rail, just as the Eurasian Landbridge today links these two great oceans across the Eurasian continent, Lincoln's economist Henry Carey and his friends promoted "encircling the world with iron," through rail projects connecting the entire world—including a bridge over the Bering Strait connecting Russia and the American continent. This project is now supported by both Russia and China, and only lacks the will on the American side to join hands for the development of all. President Putin identified the Bering Strait Bridge project as a "war avoidance" policy, capturing the concept of "Peace through Development."

At the end of World War II, President Roosevelt envisioned the use of the astonishing productive power in the United States, built to defeat fascism and militarism, put to the use of building the formerly colonized world, together with Russia and China, our wartime allies.

But Roosevelt died too soon, his weak successor Truman aided the return of the European powers to their colonies, and instead of development, we saw the continuation of colonial wars. Now, rather than joint development, we see NATO forces moving to the Russian borders in Europe, a "pivot" to Asia with the intention of bringing more U.S. warships to the Pacific, massive U.S. military power deployed into an ASEAN country, including on Palawan Island in the South China Sea, THAAD high-altitude missiles in a ring around China and the Russian Far East. Meanwhile both Russia and China, although remaining within their immediate geographic regions, are building up their military and conducting huge military exercises themselves, warning that any utopian dream of "winning" a nuclear war is pure madness, that the entire world would be destroyed.

Asian Opportunities

Yet the solution to this threat to civilization is before us here today: Xi Jinping's offer to President Obama at the 2014 APEC meeting for the United States to join in the Silk Road process, both in Eurasia and, as Helga LaRouche has proposed, in building a World Land-Bridge.

Look at Asia's leading hot spots: North Korea, the South China Sea, and the extension of Mideast terrorism into the region. In Korea, even as tensions swell and wane—and you all know that tensions are at a high point today—an extraordinary development is taking place. Three leading South Korean corporations, Hyundai Marine, POSCO, and KORAIL, have formed a joint venture with Russia and North Korea around the North Korean port of Rason (aka Rajin). Both the Russians and Chinese have built new port facilities there over the past year, with new road and rail connections to China and to Vladivostok.

Russian coal is being transported to this new port in North Korea, shipped on Hyundai ships to South Korea, then by KORAIL to POSCO steel plants. The South Korean government is also rebuilding the rail lines that lead to the border, with the intention of eventually linking South Korea to the trans-Siberian Railway through North Korea, completing the vision of the Eurasian Land-Bridge "from Pusan to Rotterdam." Only by giving the North such a stake in the transformation of all of Asia through the Silk Road process is there a chance to end the conflict peacefully.

So also in the South China Sea. China's Foreign Minister Wang Yi, speaking at the ASEAN Regional Forum in Malaysia this month, posed a "win-win" solution as part of the New Maritime Silk Road sponsored by President Xi Jinping. Minister Wang announced that the building of the new artificial islands had been completed, and that the next step is to "build facilities primarily used for public purposes, including lighthouses, maritime emergency rescue, weather stations, and marine scientific research, as well as medical and first-aid buildings. Once the construction is completed," he said, "China is willing to open these facilities to countries in the region.

As the largest coastal country in the South China Sea, China has the ability and obligation to provide these maritime public goods to countries in the region." Again, peace through development, if the world chooses it rather than war. It is of note that the western press entirely blacked out this portion of Wang Yi's speech.

FIGURE 2

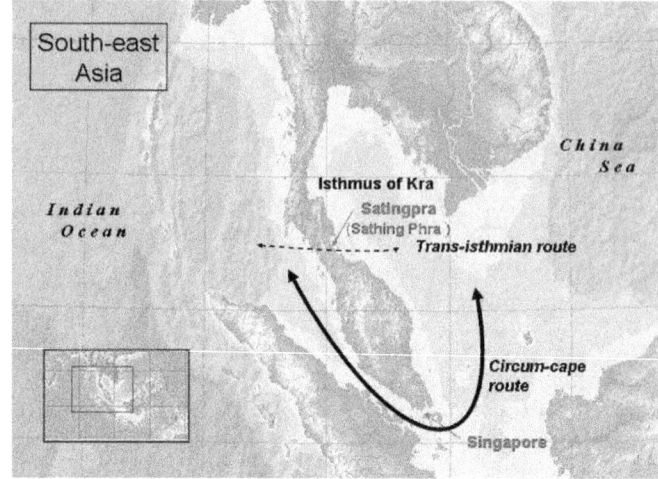

EIRNS

The proposed site of the Kra Canal

Another major project on the agenda of the New Maritime Silk Road—one which was conceived long before the building of the Panama Canal or the Suez Canal—is the Kra Canal across the Isthmus of Kra in southern Thailand. Lyndon and Helga LaRouche, in 1983 and 1984, co-sponsored with the Thai government, two symposia in Bangkok on the tremendous potential for the entire Pacific-Indian Ocean Basin of building a canal and a trade hub in southern Thailand, which would shorten the travel time in the world's busiest sea lanes, and avoid the imminent overcrowding of the Malacca Strait, while providing development to the Muslim population in the region who face economic exclusion and relative poverty, which has fed the growth of terrorist movements in the region.

Similarly, the Silk Road Economic Belt is already bringing massive development to western China and Central Asia, as a necessary precondition for ending the poverty, drugs, and isolation, which feed terrorist recruitment among the youth. The Schiller Institute has circulated a petition calling on the U.S. and Europe to reject geopolitics in favor of "win-win" cooperation with the BRICS in the New Silk Road and the Global Land-Bridge. The task facing mankind today is to see the current crisis as an opportunity for human creativity and cooperation as the necessary means to finally put war behind us, as truly impossible in the age of thermonuclear weapons, and embrace peace through development based on the common aims of mankind.